M000209265

HOW TO SELF-PUBLISH AND MARKET A CHILDREN'S BOOK

THE KEY STEPS TO SELF-PUBLISHING IN PRINT
AND AS AN EBOOK AND HOW TO GET YOUR
STORY INTO YOUNG READERS' HANDS

KAREN P INGLIS

Well Said Press
www.wellsaidpress.com

Copyright © 2018 by Karen Inglis

Published by Well Said Press 2018

83 Castelnau . London . SW13 9RT

Print Book ISBN: 978-0-9954543-4-7

ePub ISBN: 978-0-9954543-5-4

All rights reserved.

No part of this book may be reproduced in any form or by any electronic
or mechanical means, including information storage and retrieval systems,
without written permission from the author, except for the use of brief
quotations in a book review.

CONTENTS

INTRODUCTION

Welcome to *How to Self-publish and Market a Children's Book.*

Thank you for buying this book and congratulations if you've written a children's story – or are part way through your first draft. There really never has been a better time to be a writer and I can't wait to share with you what I've learned during my children's fiction self-publishing journey since 2011.

Whether you have a manuscript that you're not sure what to do with, are traditionally published or with an agent but also want to explore self-publishing, or are already self-published but in need of help with marketing, you're in the right place.

This book offers you a practical guide to:

- understanding and getting help with the tasks you need to complete before you self-publish

- turning your finished manuscript (picture book, illustrated chapter book or middle grade novel*) into a print book and eBook for the Kindle store and other eBook platforms
- getting your self-published (or indeed traditionally-published) children's book noticed and into the hands of as many young readers as possible – the holy grail for most children's authors

* middle grade novel is a US term that's being used increasingly in the UK – refers to books for ages 8-12

While 'how to write for children' is outside the scope of this book, I do touch on key aspects of this important topic and provide links to relevant books and online resources. Unless you are confident in being able to write for a younger audience, I'd highly recommend reading one or more of those recommended resources alongside this book.

And although this book focuses on self-publishing children's fiction, the processes and marketing methods will, of course, work or can be adapted equally well for children's non-fiction.

Learning curves and challenges

Self-publishing production tasks involve a few learning curves, but don't be too concerned. The platforms and tools at your disposal are, for the most part, very user-friendly (a far cry from when I started self-publishing back in 2011!) and there are armies of specialist freelancers out there, ready to help when you need them.

Marketing will be your main challenge. With children's books the opportunities we have – and the pathways to our readers – differ from what's available to authors who write for adult or even young adult (YA) audiences. That means we need to do some things differently, and put in more time and more thought. It is hard work, but the rewards of being able to share your story with hundreds or even thousands of children at home and abroad more than make up for it!

PART I

SELF-PUBLISHING

MY SELF-PUBLISHING JOURNEY

When I first started out, it was never my intention to self-publish – indeed it wasn't even an option when I wrote the first drafts of my children's books back when my two boys were toddlers. Like most other authors, I went through the process of identifying suitable publishers and agents, sending out my manuscripts (always by post in those days) and getting back polite rejections six or seven weeks later.

Early rejections and near misses

I had three books rejected back in those days: a set of rhyming stories about a friendly urban fox called Ferdinand, my historical time travel adventure *The Secret Lake* and a humorous chapter book about a soccer-mad runaway alien called 'Eeek!'

In the case of my *Ferdinand Fox* stories I was told that rhyming stories had very little chance of being picked up unless you were already a household name. This is because rhyming text limits the ability to sell foreign rights (due to the translation issue), which in turn limits the ability to arrange printing in large enough numbers in the same run (called co-editions) to bring down the colour print cost.

With *The Secret Lake* I was told that the story, while very well written, was 'too traditional', and in some cases 'too short' and/or that children were looking for something 'more modern' – or simply that the publisher's list was already full.

I had my closest shave with *Eeek! The Runaway Alien*, which received compliments from the then Children's Senior Commissioning editor at Bloomsbury (little did I know that she was then working on the first Harry Potter book!). She said that she had really enjoyed the story and my 'light and natural' writing style but that *Eeek!* was too short for their standalone lists and too long for a series read. So, again, it didn't quite fit. She did ask for more ideas and examples of my writing, which was very encouraging, but it came to nothing. Following a few more close shaves with agents, I decided that my chances of getting selected were very slim, so went back to my day job of copywriting and business writing training.

After that, my stories sat on my hard drive and in a wooden box in my office for 10 years. During that very busy period I would occasionally glance at that box and think what a pity it was that no one would ever discover the characters and adventures that lay locked in there!

Discovering Amazon CreateSpace – taking control

It was only when I pulled my stories out during a year-long sabbatical from my consultancy work in 2010, that I began to hear and read about Amazon's CreateSpace self-publishing platform. The more I read (I spent hours in the CreateSpace and other community forums learning about the nuts and bolts of self-publishing from formatting and printing gurus), the more I decided this was for me.

Nearly all the self-publishing authors I knew of at that time were based in the States (apart from Joanna Penn, now UK-based but then in Australia – do google her if you don't know her) and all were writing for adults. But that didn't put me off. More than anything it was the **control** this option gave me that was most appealing. Not just the **creative control** over my work – the themes, format and length of my stories – but also **control over when and how I could publish** my work.

I have to confess that I hadn't given the marketing side of things a second thought at that stage – it would be a challenge to face and overcome later on.

Since self-publishing

The figures and anecdotes I share overleaf demonstrate what is possible if you decide to self-publish and are prepared to put in the hard work both before and after your story goes to print. All figures are as at July 2018. (I should add that I know of plenty of self-published children's authors who have outsold me.)

If you have a great story, and follow the key advice in this book – both at the pre-publishing and the marketing stage – you have just as good a chance of getting your book into hundreds if not thousands of children's hands.

The Secret Lake

- Over 9,500 sales in print
- Almost 4,000 Kindle/eBook sales
- Praised by librarians, teachers, reading charities and parents for its manageable length
- Considered for adaptation by Children's BBC TV after being read by CBBC Head of Independent Commissioning
- Over 50 5-Star reviews Amazon UK/USA
- Still my top seller at school events
- Hit several Amazon UK children's bestseller lists (print and Kindle store) in Summer 2018

Eeek! The Runaway Alien

- Selected as *LoveReading4Kids* Book of the Month at publication (a highly regarded UK children's book recommendation site)
- Used for Years 2 and 3 literacy projects (2012, 2013, 2016)
- Unsolicited requests for school visits
- Received over £450 in royalties from schools copying – ongoing
- Unsolicited requests for reading copies from mainstream publishers in Turkey and Germany

- Over 2,800 print sales
- Used in the *Get London Reading* campaign

Ferdinand Fox's Big Sleep

- Over 900 print sales
- Shipped 17 copies to Cyprus in 2018 following a Skype school visit request

Ferdinand Fox and the Hedgehog

- Over 800 print sales
- One online purchase has led to two whole-school visits in Hereford in autumn 2018

Henry Haynes and the Great Escape

- 950 print sales
- Extremely popular with early readers!

Walter Brown and the Magician's Hat

- Over 650 print sales
- Red Ribbon Winner Wishing Shelf Book Awards 2016 (judged by children and teachers in six UK primary schools)

Making a living from my books

I don't earn enough from my books alone to live on, but they do provide an increasing contribution. The same could be true for you – just don't give up the day job unless you can afford to! Of course, you could strike lucky and become the next indie author whose sales go through the roof – but until then, don't look at self-publishing as a quick route to riches. According to a survey by the Authors Licensing and Collecting Society, the median annual income of UK professional writers (including authors) was below £10,500 in 2017 – a drop of 15% in real terms since 2013. There's no further breakdown available for this at the time of writing, but I wouldn't be surprised if that income figure is quite a bit lower for the average mid-list children's author.

What self-publishing does offer, however, is a much faster way to get your book into your readers' hands.

I hope this gives you a flavour of what self-publishing can offer for you.

Quick note August 2018: CreateSpace is currently being phased out with all authors being migrated to a parallel platform called KDP Print - I cover this throughout the book.

2

SELF-PUBLISHING FAQS

Is it better to be traditionally published?

That really depends on how you measure success. Back in the very early days I might have said 'yes', because at that time I measured success in books sales alone. At that time self-publishing was viewed largely as vanity publishing, and associated with poor quality writing and editing – no matter how well-written and edited your book actually was. As a self-publisher, the prospect of ever selling many books felt remote as getting into bookshops and literary events, being able to enter competitions, or to submit your book for reviews to established reviewers and bloggers was an uphill struggle.

However, in the last five years the self-publishing industry has matured, with organisations such as **The Alliance of Independent Authors** championing professionalism at each stage of the process, helping change attitudes of both authors and the wider publishing and book-selling industry. At the same time, new formatting tools, collaborative platforms and digital advertising solutions have evolved, making it easier for self-publishers to produce top quality books in partnership with freelance experts, and to find their readers online and face to face. Thus, many of the earlier challenges of self-publishing have fallen away, making selling books in good (and even large) numbers a realistic possibility if you work hard at it.

On this basis I'd say that neither approach is better than the other and the choice then becomes one of how much control you want over your work – both creative control and over the timing of getting your book to market. If you want the backing of an established publisher and are happy to wait as long as that takes, then the traditional publishing route may be better for you. However, if you've tried without success, or want to get your book into readers' hands sooner rather than later, then self-publishing is your friend.

I should, though, mention that in the area of foreign rights self-publishers are only nibbling at the edges just now – and it's an area that I'd happily hand over to someone else if there were a path. At present this isn't easy without the backing of a mainstream publisher, though I'm confident that this area will mature and change over time. If it's a top priority for you, then traditional publishing is the way to go.

Will I sell lots of books if I self-publish?

There is no magic bullet with self-publishing. The life-changing success stories you may have read about (which, by the way, nearly all relate to authors who write for adults or, very occasionally, young adults) are the exception rather than the rule. But if you work hard and follow the advice in this book you stand as good a chance as the next author of selling in reasonable numbers.

SELF-PUBLISHING OPTIONS: 'DIY' OR OUTSOURCE?

You have two main choices with self-publishing:

- **'DIY'** – where you manage the key tasks yourself, hiring in freelancers along the way, then upload your book files, and monitor sales and royalties directly. This is the preferred method for most self-publishers as it is the most cost effective, and gives you direct control over your work for sales and marketing purposes – as will be seen later.

- **'Assisted Publishing'** – either 'full package' (where you pay someone to manage everything for you, from editing right through to upload, royalty gathering and marketing), or 'self-select package' (my terminology for convenience) where you choose from a menu of services that they manage for you.

As you can see, 'DIY' doesn't mean you will do everything

yourself – far from it. And there are key tasks where third-party input is a must, such as editing, proofreading and (for most) illustration. It's up to you whether you DIY or outsource the more technical tasks such as formatting – but they are all within your direct control.

The chapters that follow – and which make up most of the first half of this book – focus on the 'DIY' self-publishing approach, as this is the preferred method for most independent authors. I cover assisted publishing in Chapter 10.

BEFORE YOU SELF-PUBLISH

Self-publishing isn't a way to cut corners and race to market. It's in your interests to make sure that you do everything you can **before you self-publish** to ensure that your finished manuscript is the best it possibly can be.

Serious children's self-publishers follow the same steps as traditional publishers in making sure that their stories are engaging and relevant for their target readers, well-written and use appropriate language. That's not to say that you'll please everyone – children of all ages have different tastes. But there are key steps to follow both before and after putting pen to paper – and most certainly before deciding to hit the 'self-publish' button to ensure that your book is as good as it can be.

I've listed those high-level steps below and provided additional resources for you to refer to where necessary. If you have a finished manuscript and haven't already followed these steps, it's highly likely that you are not yet ready to take your story out into the big wide world. If that is the case I'd hit the pause button and plug any gaps that need filling from below.

1. Research phase

Understanding what makes a good children's story

What makes a good children's story is outside the scope of this book – however, as with all fiction writing, it hinges around:

- an engaging or compelling story or plot, with associated twists, turns, surprises, conflicts or set-backs along the way
- believable characters with whom the reader can empathise or identify as they accompany them on their physical and emotional journey – whether or not they like them
- a satisfying end (which ideally has the reader champing at the bit for the next book if it's a series read, or will send them scurrying to look out what else you may have written if it's not)
- quality illustrations that complement or enhance the text (picture books or illustrated chapter books)

This applies from the simplest picture book to the most complex of middle grade novels. In short, it must engage and entertain your reader (be that the child or the parent and child) from the first page until the last.

Overleaf are a few recommendations and suggestions if you want to understand more about writing for children.

WRITING FOR CHILDREN RESOURCE LIST

- *How to write for children and get published – Louise Jordan* Louise was head reader at Puffin UK for 20+ years and now runs WritersAdvice.co.uk

- *How to write a children's book – Kate Davis* Although I've not read this, the author has good credentials. Worth sampling on Kindle.

- *How to Write a Children's Picture Book (book series) – Eve Heidi Bine-Stock* Great on structure.

- *The making of a picture book – Stephen Davies (blog post series) –* bit.ly/makingPB

- *Joyce Dunbar's guide to writing picture books – (blog post) –* bit.ly/JoyceDunbar

- *How to write a children's book – Darcy Pattison (online course) –* bit.ly/DarcyCourse

You'll find this list and other suggestions with links at: selfpublishingadventures.com/resources using the password found in Chapter 29.

Knowing your target market

With children's books planning is crucial – not least because children's tastes, reading ability and 'staying power' with a story vary by age and other factors. For that reason, it's vital that you **know what age you're writing for** then **target your book accordingly**. Everything flows from here – the language, the book length, the themes. Get that first bit wrong and you'll find yourself falling at the first hurdle.

So – where do you start?

Whether you only have a kernel of an idea for a children's book, a work-in-progress or a finished manuscript, I'd start by asking myself what age it's aimed at. I'd then go to my local library and get out as many books for that age group as I can and read them. I'd also read either side of that age group to get a feel for the subtle changes in language, story complexity, and themes.

Take note of typical page counts, words per page, font sizes and line spacing, number and form of illustrations for different age ranges. This will show you the word count (range) you should be aiming for – and help inform later decisions about book size and interior style and layout.

Thankfully with self-publishing you will not be bound by what mainstream publishers require in order to 'fit their lists', but children of a certain age will generally be looking for books of a certain length (and for younger readers a certain style and/or frequency of illustrations) – and ideally you want your book to sit comfortably with others on the bookshelves.

The above said, keep an open mind. Reluctant readers will often prefer a shorter book with shorter chapters, so if you're targeting your story at this audience check out the specific competition (your librarian, local children's bookseller or a

Google search will help you with this). Will that style and length fit your story idea? Or does your already-finished manuscript feel about right?

This research stage is crucial in assuring there will be a market for your book. If you find that you're off the mark with your idea or your current manuscript, you will at least have plenty of ideas to help you reshape it, whether by adapting it for a different age group, or by adjusting the language/story/length/theme/illustrations to make it more appropriate for the target age range.

CHILDREN'S BOOKS TYPICAL AGE RANGE AND WORD COUNT IN THE UK

- **Picture book (0-5yrs)** 0-1000 (average 500)
- **Chapter book (5-7yrs)** 1,000-6,000
- **Middle grade novel (8-12yrs)** 20,000-40,000

Note that my illustrated middle grade novel *Eeek! The Runaway Alien* for ages 7-10 (popular with both keen and reluctant readers) is only 15,000 words, so don't get too hung up on these numbers!

Part of the joy of being an indie author is the flexibility it offers you.

Next steps

With your research phase complete you're in a strong position to start planning and drafting your story – far more so than would have been the case had you simply sat down and started to write!

2. Planning and early drafts phase

Creating your first draft

Some writers are 'plotters' and map out their story from start to finish before starting to write, while others are 'pantsers', meaning they have an idea of their story's main characters and plot, but tend to write by the seat of their pants. Having tried both methods, I would highly recommend at least some level of plotting before you start – experience has shown me that it saves a lot of time and confusion down the line, not least when time travel is involved! *The Secret Lake* took me double the number of drafts of my later books because I didn't have a detailed plan!

Below are a few useful books and courses about structure and plotting, just in case you're not sure where to start. These don't all focus on children's books and some relate to screen writing but that really doesn't matter.

BOOKS FOCUS

- Plotting Your Novel: Ideas and Structure – Janice Hardy
- Plot and Structure – James Scott Bell
- Story Genius – Lisa Cron
- The Magic Words – Cheryl B Klein (children's / YA)

SCREENWRITING FOCUS

- Save the Cat – Blake Snyder
- Into the Woods – John Yorke
- Inside Story – Dara Marks

- Story – Robert McKee

I read 'Story' by Robert McKee before I first started writing – a brilliant in-depth resource not to be missed. It's a tome, so I'd suggest tackling this after something shorter!

PAID FACE-TO-FACE COURSES (LONDON, UK)

- Children's writing courses (various, including plotting) – City Lit Adult Education, Covent Garden

FREE ONLINE RESOURCES/COURSES

- Future Learn – free course examining fairy tale themes and structure
- How to plot with the three-act structure – Janice Hardy
- Screenwriting Tricks for Authors – Alexandra Sokoloff
- Story Engines (taster online training) – Joe Nassise, introduction from Nick Stephenson

You'll find this list with links in the resources area at: selfpublishingadventures.com/resources using the password found in Chapter 29.

Chapter book or picture book first drafts

For **illustrated chapter books,** hold off talking to an illustrator (or doing your own illustrations) during this first draft stage. Rather, insert comments or placeholder frames within the text to describe where an image will appear and what it will show. That way, if the first feedback phase says your story isn't working you won't have wasted time or expense on illustrations that may not be needed or will need adjusting.

Similarly, with **picture book first drafts**, just use placeholder frames with notes or pin-man sketches until you've tested the story with your target audience using a mock-up.

I cover all of this in more detail, including how to create a storyboard and picture book mock-up, in Chapter 7, *'Print book design – planning and resources'*.

Leaving your manuscript to rest

Whichever method you use, once your first draft is complete and as good as you feel you can make it, put it to one side for a week or two to 'rest' then take a second look. You'll be surprised by how taking a step away can help you spot plot weaknesses or poor writing to which you were previously blind.

It's highly likely that you'll need to do further editing after this 'pause' but don't be downhearted – it's all part of the process and every good writer goes through it.

Next steps

By the end of this phase you will have your first draft, self-edited to a stage that you feel ready to show it around. This will be the first of several stages of taking in feedback. (As mentioned above, Chapter 7 provides more detail on how to prepare for the early feedback phase that follows.)

3. Early feedback phase

Beta readers

Once your manuscript is complete, 'rested' and has had any final edits, now's the time to get initial feedback. You could go straight to an editor, but it's more cost effective at this stage to find some **beta readers** (test readers), including children, from at least two of the following groups:

- children in your target age range – ideally most of whom don't know you!
- children's librarians
- primary/nursery teachers
- other writers who have an interest in children's books
- children's booksellers

This needn't cost you anything. However, in return for their feedback **offer them a free signed copy of your book once it's out**. (This will also give you a chance to request a review later down the line when you send them your book – every little helps at launch, as you will later find out!) Parents and teachers will be able to pass the book on and the children themselves will be thrilled to receive a dedicated signed copy. In the case of booksellers (eg from a local bookshop), you could offer to host a signing event once your book is out.

I'd say between five and 10 readers is sufficient, with at least two adults in the mix. For the children, include a simple questionnaire (I provide an example on page 25), carefully worded to ensure you will understand from their answers which parts of the book may or may not be working.

Places to find beta readers

- Approach your local library and ask if you can leave flyers at the desk – this worked well for me with *The Secret Lake,* garnering me seven children and the librarian herself.
- Ask teachers at your local school and / or the local school librarian / children's bookseller – again provide a flyer.
- Parents outside the school gates – but go early before the children emerge.
- Facebook groups frequented by parents, or parenting sites such as Mumsnet (or the equivalent in your country) – but take care not to appear to be 'promoting' your book. This generally doesn't go down well.
- Local toddler groups – for picture books.
- Facebook groups for avid readers of children's books – but again judge it carefully and avoid appearing to be there simply to promote.
- Writers / writing groups with an interest in children's books.

For tips on how to create an attractive flyer for free using a program called **Canva**, see Chapter 20. The software is very easy to use and you can print the flyers off at home or locally.

EXAMPLE FEEDBACK QUESTIONNAIRE

Keep your questionnaire reasonably simple – short enough to ensure that busy young readers complete it, but also worded to get the answers you need, not least where the story is and isn't working.

On the opposite page you'll see a screenshot of the questionnaire I sent to the eight children who read the first draft of *Walter Brown and the Magician's Hat* for me – which, at that time, had another title.

I found these volunteers via a school I had visited a couple of years earlier. Their teacher set them the 'read and review' work over the October half-term break, which was perfect. Thankfully, their replies were consistent enough to let me know that the story didn't have any major flaws – what did surprise me, however, was that they nearly all voted for the alternative book title!

Clearly you need to adapt the format shown onto an A4 / US Letter page and leave space for the answers. This means it's likely to run to two pages.

For picture books, or any other book where the adult is reading, you could adapt this or use it as-is, or just ask for free-form feedback.

Walter Brown and the **Flaming Fire Fiend**
(NB: the final version will include black and white illustrations.)

Feedback questionnaire – please be honest as it helps the author ☺

1. **How much did you enjoy the story? Please choose:**

   I enjoyed it   I loved it   It was ok   I didn't really enjoy it

2. **Another title idea is 'Walter Brown and the Magician's Hat' - which title do you prefer? This one or the other one?**

3. **If you didn't enjoy the story or just thought it was ok (or if you stopped reading it) can you say what you didn't enjoy about it and where you stopped reading?** *(Leave blank if this doesn't apply to you.)*

4. **What was your favourite part (or parts) of the story?**

5. **Was there anything you didn't understand about what happened or found confusing?**

6. **Did any of the story feel boring or slow? If 'Yes' which part?**

7. **Who was your favourite character or characters? (say why if you like!)**

8. **The attached cover is just one idea for the book - what do you think? Would it make you want to pick up the book if you saw it in a bookshop? If you think it could be better, how might you change it? Thank you for your feedback** ☺

Also view in the resources folder.

Questions along the lines of those above should work for most chapter books through to middle grade novels.

My readers were aged 7-8 so I kept it relatively simple. You could certainly embellish/add in extras to get more detailed feedback if your test readers are at the top end of the middle grade age range, ie ages 10-12.

However, keep in mind that if you make it too involved you risk getting nothing back!

Formatting and sending your manuscript to beta readers

PRINT READING COPIES

Most children read in print, so I'd recommend offering this format as default. However, a wad of A4 pages can look off-putting, so present the text as an A5 booklet in Word or PDF, to give the closest reading experience to a book that you can (the Word instructions on creating an A5 booklet are easy to follow). For chapter books, you could even insert placeholder frames to show where any images are likely to appear. In this case, choose a font size and line spacing that's broadly in keeping with books for your target audience, which you should have worked out during the research phase. For picture books you will, of course, be using your mock-ups. As these will be quick to read, you could perhaps pass one or two around rather than making one for every reader. (I cover image planning and mock-ups in Chapter 7.)

KINDLE READING COPIES

Some adults or older children may prefer (or be happy) to read your early draft on their Kindle. If so, it's easy to email them a Word document which will magically appear ready to read on their device. For this to work they need to 'allow' their Kindle to accept an email from you. This is easy to set up, but they probably won't know how. I provide a step-by-step guide for this in *'Tips and tools for sending eBook review copies'* in Chapter 22 in the marketing section.

USING BOOKFUNNEL TO DISTRIBUTE EBOOKS

Another way you can distribute your manuscript in eBook form is using an excellent and very reasonably priced subscription service called *BookFunnel* – though this is probably more suitable for when you are into your second book or well into your marketing phase on the first. Again, I cover this, in *'Tips and tools for sending eBook review copies'* in the marketing section.

Next steps

Armed with your first level of feedback you are now ready to rewrite/restructure and/or polish your manuscript further before seeking feedback from a professional editor.

4. Professional review and editing

Why do I need an editor?

As I mentioned at the start, serious self-publishers follow the same process as traditional publishers when it comes to manuscript preparation. To ignore this step is a false economy – we are all too close to our writing to recognise when something isn't working. Without an editor's input we risk publishing stories with glaring flaws or substandard writing – or, even worse, both! If JK Rowling and Roald Dahl used editors for their books, why on earth would any of us think we can do without?!

A children's fiction editor who specialises in your genre will ensure that your book is the best it possibly can be in terms of:

- how well the overall story works for its target audience

- whether the language is appropriate for the reading age
- whether the themes covered are suitable for the age range
- the quality, flow and consistency of your writing

Through their comments they will also teach you huge amounts about writing that you can apply in your next story.

The key levels of editing

There are a variety of terms in use to describe the different levels of editing, but they broadly fall into three categories: structural review, copy editing (or line editing), and proofing. If you have the budget I would recommend using all three. If you really don't have the budget and have been meticulous in taking on beta reader feedback, then at the very least use the services of a copy editor, followed by proofreading.

(1) STRUCTURAL REVIEW (SOMETIMES CALLED 'DEVELOPMENTAL EDIT' OR 'MANUSCRIPT APPRAISAL')

An experienced children's book editor will give you comprehensive feedback on your story in terms of its structure, pace, storyline, setting, characters/character development and suitability of language/dialogue. In short, they will identify whether the story works in and of itself and for the intended age group. Some may also pick up glaring grammar or copywriting edits along the way – but that will depend on how much work they have to do at the higher structural level.

You may ask whether this step is necessary if you've already tested your manuscript with beta readers and revised it in response. My answer would be a resounding **yes**. I received high-level professional editorial feedback on all of my titles after testing them out with children and adults, and the input took the stories to another level. In the case of *The Secret Lake* it also prevented me making some beginner mistakes that I knew not to repeat in my later books.

Not only does a structural review force you to deal with those elements of your story that you probably knew all along weren't quite working (or could be improved) but – and here's the bonus – it teaches you bucket loads about what makes good writing. It's like a crash course in writing for children. And because you are in there 'at the coalface' responding to this advice, you remember and take what you learn with you – ready to apply to your next book. Absorbing and acting on this feedback will help your storytelling mature more quickly and, over time, will reduce the amount of reworking needed in subsequent manuscripts. In short, it will make you a better writer all round – perhaps even allowing you to roll the structural and copy-editing stages into one for later books.

(Note that some authors separate out 'manuscript appraisal' from structural review – to all intents and purposes they amount to the same thing, with the manuscript appraisal being perhaps a higher-level commentary.)

(II) Copy editing (or 'line editing')

The job of a copy editor is more one of detail and polishing – they are not there to suggest wholesale changes to your story, as by now that should have been taken care of. Rather, they will read your manuscript for consistency and accuracy – largely focusing on readability, writing style and grammar. They are also there to pick up on factual inaccuracies (use of names, places, real world facts etc) or inconsistencies within the plot line (such as getting names, setting, timing – or even character traits – wrong based on what's gone before). As a matter of course, they are likely to pick out glaring proofing errors, but don't count on it!

(III) PROOFING

The final step is the proofreading stage and while it may be very tempting to think this is where you can save money, I would strongly recommend paying for at least one extra pair of eyes to proofread both your final manuscript and your print proof.

By way of example, after line-by-line proofing of my final Word manuscript of *The Secret Lake* – followed by further checking by my husband, my eagle-eyed mother and a writing colleague – I was convinced I had my proofing all sewn up for very little outlay. More fool me! When my first print proof arrived from CreateSpace I found that it still contained close to 20 errors, from basic typos to missing words to incorrect spacing issues. Yes, I was able to catch those – but once the book was out there, a further five or six errors surfaced. Had I used a professional proofreader I'm pretty sure most of these would have been picked up at the final proof stage.

On this basis I'd say that when it comes to your final proofing, ideally pick someone who's not read the story already. I may be wrong, but my instinct is that someone who knows the story already is more likely to drop their guard and pass over mistakes as they settle into the familiar routine of your tale.

Where to find editors and proofreaders

Below are a couple of my personal recommendations. However, new services are springing up all the time, particularly as more editors who have worked for mainstream publishers are offering their services to indie authors on a freelance basis. As well as checking these out, search online and – above all – ask fellow children's writers for recommendations.

The Writers' Advice Centre for Children's Books

The Writers' Advice Centre – which I highly recommend – has been offering manuscript appraisal services, advice and training to children's writers since 1994.

Its founder, Louise Jordan, was a reader for Puffin for over 20 years, and as their service has grown she has built a team of highly experienced freelance children's editors around her, all from the traditional publishing world. On this basis, if you're keeping your options open about going the traditional publishing route you are getting your work in front of people with very good connections. Moreover, Louise has recently set up her own imprint *Wacky Bee* and is always on the look-out for new authors of books for ages 5-12, so no harm done there!

The Writers' Advice Centre feedback to me on the first drafts of *The Secret Lake, Ferdinand Fox, Eeek! The Runaway Alien* and *Walter Brown and the Magician's Hat* was invaluable and I've carried much of that with my writing today. They offer:

WRITTEN APPRAISAL SERVICE

- available for completed or part-completed manuscripts
- charges range from £100 up to £400 at the time of writing, depending on word count – see *writersadvice.co.uk* for full details
- an assigned editor prepares a detailed and "frank" (this is important!) report on your manuscript, typically within 30 days
- the report covers presentation, targeting, subject matter, theme, plotting, structure, style, characterisation, dialogue, viewpoint, approach, and a suggested list of further reading

TELEPHONE APPRAISAL SERVICE

- one-to-one telephone advice from Louise Jordan (Managing Editor of Writers' Advice) on a completed or part-completed piece of writing up to a maximum of 25,000 words
- choice of a general discussion on your story / story idea without sending in a manuscript, or specific feedback on a manuscript sent in in advance
- you choose which aspects of your manuscript you'd like to discuss – or you can request general feedback

- prices at the time of writing are £30 plus reading fee for a 15-minute call or £60 plus reading fee for a 30-minute call – reading fee depends on manuscript length – see *writersadvice.co.uk* for more details
- two-week turnaround promised where manuscript sent in

FACE-TO-FACE EDITORIAL MEETING

- one-to-one with Louise Jordan
- may be a general discussion, a tutorial, or to look at a specific piece of work (up to a maximum of 25,000 words)
- manuscripts of more than 1,000 words need sending in advance
- prices at the time of writing range from £80 for up to 1,000 words, to £305 for 25,000 words (including the advance reading fee) – see *writersadvice.co.uk* for more details

COPY EDITING SERVICE

- prices at the time of writing from £200 – submit your manuscript for a 'no obligation' quote
- fee will vary based on length of manuscript and the complexity/nature of edits required – from simple corrections, grammar and spelling, through to a complete restructuring of manuscript content

Find out more at **writersadvice.co.uk**

Reedsy

Reedsy offers a global online marketplace of editorial (amongst others) professionals, all of whom come from a traditional publishing background and have been vetted by Reedsy. Here's how it works:

- You can search by middle grade, picture book or YA/teen editor.
- You can also search based on English language editing style – British, US, Australian, South African etc
- Each editor has a profile outlining their previous editorial/publishing experience, the types of editing service they offer and which types of children's books they have worked on.
- Attached to each profile there is a customer review system – where authors have rated and commented on the service they received.
- You can request quotes online from several editors at the same time, by supplying a project brief and book sample.
- Each editor sets their own price and Reedsy takes a modest commission based on what you pay.
- Reedsy also offers useful tips on how to choose the right editor.

I successfully used Reedsy to find an experienced editor (ex-Harper Collins) for *Walter Brown and the Magician's Hat*. Her feedback was invaluable and taught me a huge amount about plot, pace and character arc – worth every penny!

Reedsy also offers access to design, formatting, marketing and PR professionals – as well as a range of free writing tools and training resources.

Find out more at **www.Reedsy.com/a/inglis**

(Tip: If you sign up with my affiliate link above you'll get a $20 credit to use against your first project. In return I will earn a small introductory fee by way of thanks for the recommendation.)

Alliance of Independent Authors' Self-Publishing Services Directory

The Alliance of Independent Authors (ALLi) – which I would highly recommend joining – has a directory of vetted professionals offering a range of self-publishing services including editing, print and eBook formatting, cover design and more. Most offer ALLi members a discount for their services – typically 10-25%, but often more.

At the time of writing I'm not sure how many specialise in children's books editing, but the list of providers is constantly updated. Editing apart, it's certainly worth a look for other services, such as illustration and cover design, which I cover in Chapter 7.

The directory is free to download for members of ALLi – or anyone can view it online at: **bit.ly/ALLiDirectory**

However, to benefit from the partner member discounts you need to join ALLi. See Chapter 28 for more information on the benefits of joining and how to sign up.

Next steps

Once your book has been edited and proofread, you're ready to start your remaining self-publishing tasks, namely: cover design, interior layout, any interior illustrations, front and back matter content and formatting.

I cover each of the above aspects in Chapter 7, *'Print book design – planning and resources'* and Chapter 8, *'EBooks'*. Before moving on, however, it's important that you understand your key choices for self-publishing in print (the format of choice for children's reading) and the files you will need to create, as I will reference these when talking about specs needed for covers, book sizes and illustrations.

If you're already familiar with these options, and are certain you understand which combinations of self-publishing platform to use in parallel, feel free to skip the next chapter. If not, read on!

5

SELF-PUBLISHING IN PRINT: KEY OPTIONS

In this chapter we'll look at:

- why print matters with children's self-publishing
- recommended platforms for self-publishing in print
- the difference between print on demand and up-front print runs
- the files you will need for upload

Why print matters in children's self-publishing

As I mentioned briefly in the introduction, the runaway success stories you may have read about in self-publishing relate almost entirely to books for **adults or YA** (young adults). Many of these will have started out as impulse purchases of **eBook**s as a result of a compelling cover, great blurb, decent reviews and an attractive price point following targeted advertising or social media marketing – with the ensuing snowball effect. (As many of us know, buying eBooks on a whim is somehow so much easier than ordering in print!)

With children's books, the story is different. Your chances of selling huge numbers of eBooks are small because most children read in print – and most parents and grandparents read to their children and grandchildren in print. And where they do buy eBooks, gaining from impulse purchases is much harder than for adult/YA books, because your buyer isn't the reader – it's the parent or grandparent who will often be searching based on a child's request, a household name children's author or someone else's recommendation.

Print vs eBook in the UK Market

On the page opposite are a few facts and figures from Nielsen's UK *'Understanding the Children's Book Consumer'* 2017 report.

You can also view the table at:
selfpublishingadventures.com/resources using the password found in Chapter 29.

Volume and value of UK children's book purchases for ages 0-17 by format 2017		
	Volume	Value
All formats	**103 million**	**£599 million**
Print	96 million	£557 million
eBook	4 million	£ 23 million
Audiobook	3 million	£ 19 million

Book formats enjoyed by reading age (not mutually exclusive)		
End reader age	**Print**	**Digital (eBook/Audio)***
0-4	95%	27%
5-10	95%	30%
11-17	80%	22%

*2017 figures show a rise in audio popularity and a slight fall in eBook popularity compared with previous years though this is a one-year snapshot

Reason for liking print books	Percentage of respondents
Look and feel	48%
Easier to read	40%
Easier to find	34%
Provides a break from technology	33%
Like objects	32%

Source all figures above: Nielsen's UK 'Understanding the Children's Book Consumer' 2017 report.

Print vs eBook in the US Market

While I don't have detailed equivalent statistics for the US, a quick online search confirms what I've heard anecdotally, namely that print also rules for children's books in the US. For example:

- Children's print books were ranked second based on sales volume in the US for the last nine months of 2017. Children's eBooks didn't even make the top 10 for eBooks sales. *(Author Earnings, Jan 2018 report).*

- Sales of print children's books dominated over eBooks sales in 2016, with children's eBooks accounting for only 9% of all fiction and 1% of all nonfiction sales. Older children also favoured print –

with hard cover print books outperforming e-Reader sales for this group in 2016 for first time in six years.

- Sales of children's print books rose 3% in 2017 including an 11% year-on-year growth in board books and 20% growth in graphic novels. Earlier research had confirmed that parents favoured the tactile experience of board books for younger children over the convenience of e-Readers.

(Source: Publisher's Weekly and NPD BookScan)

To sum up, print is still 'king' when it comes to children's self-publishing – there is no fast-track to fortune with eBooks as has happened for some authors of books for adults or young adults.

The above said, eBooks still have an important role to play in your overall marketing strategy. And they still account for large numbers of absolute sales – so should not be ignored. I cover all of this in the marketing section.

For now, let's get back to print…

DIY Self-publishing – print on demand

While there are a number of options in the market for DIY self-publishing in print, below I outline the tried and tested combination of services that I recommend, and which is used by many independent authors. It requires minimal up-front cost/risk and uses 'print on demand' – meaning your book only gets printed when a customer orders it.

This combination of services is:

- **Amazon CreateSpace/KDP Print** – for listing and distributing your book on Amazon's stores worldwide (KDP stands for *Kindle Direct Publishing*)

- **Ingram Spark** – for listing and distributing your book to most other online and bricks and mortar bookshops worldwide, either directly or via wholesalers

If your children's book sales really take off and you have a strong marketing campaign, you could choose to order larger volume up-front print runs direct from printing companies. I cover this option at the end of this chapter under *'Alternatives to print on demand'*.

1. Amazon CreateSpace/KDP Print – for Amazon worldwide distribution

Both CreateSpace and KDP Print are owned by Amazon. CreateSpace has been part of Amazon since 2005, whereas KDP Print is a relatively new parallel service that's likely to replace CreateSpace in the near future, with late 2018/early 2019 seeming likely.

At the time of writing you can sign up to either service, though CreateSpace users are being encouraged to migrate files to KDP Print. On this basis I'd recommend using KDP Print out of the two. The user experience is pretty much identical apart from the fact that, using KDP Print, you can view your paperback and Kindle sales reports in one place instead of needing to sign in to two different platforms. I shall refer to them in parallel for the remainder of this book but don't be surprised if CreateSpace disappears somewhere down the line.

Amazon CreateSpace being phased out over time

KDP Print is part of Kindle Direct Publishing and Amazon

How CreateSpace/KDP Print works – at a glance

1. You upload your book's fully formatted interior file and (separate) cover file to the CreateSpace/KDP platform – **there is no cost to do this, nor to list on Amazon**.
2. Within 48-72 hours your book's page – including the thumbnail of the front cover – will appear on all Amazon stores and the title will show as 'In Stock'.
3. When a customer orders your book, Amazon will print it 'on demand' and ship it to that customer. You don't need to do anything.

During upload you:

- confirm which Amazon stores (and other online retailers, if relevant) you wish to distribute to
- set your price and see what your royalty will be (you can flex the figures on-screen using their calculators before finalising your prices)
- write your book description – this will appear on your book's Amazon page
- choose which two main categories you wish your book to appear in on Amazon (you can add more later)
- choose up to seven key word search terms to help readers discover your book
- review an online proof of your book once the file has processed – you can re-upload as many times as you wish if you find any errors
- order a physical proof once you're happy with the online proof – there is a small charge for this
- approve your book for sale once you've checked and are happy with the physical (printed) proof

Making corrections or changes

If you discover an error in your book, or decide you want to change the cover at any stage, it's quick and easy to replace the files. And – best of all – it's free! Changes normally appear within 48-72 hours. During the changeover period, a CreateSpace book will show as 'temporarily out of stock', albeit still available to order. With KDP Print it will continue to show in stock at all times – clearly a better option.

Royalty rates for CreateSpace/KDP Print books

Amazon takes 40% of your chosen recommended retail price (RRP) then adds a fixed charge plus a 'per page' charge. The total is deducted from your RRP and what's left is your profit/royalty. These deductions and charges cover Amazon's production and printing costs – and, of course, allow them some profit on top.

In practice this means that the royalty rate you can earn on each print book will depend on:

- page count
- paper size (book size)
- printing format – colour or black and white interior
- the recommended retail price you set for it

With my children's print books I'm earning around 30% of my recommended retail price on Amazon and I'd say that most self-published authors are earning between 20%-30%. This compares favourably with more typical rates of 7-10% in the traditionally published world after any advance has been earned out.

Sales and royalty reports

Each sale that you make is listed on your dashboard – along with the date of the sale, the Amazon store in which the sale was made, and the royalty due to you. CreateSpace royalties are paid approximately 30 days after the month of sale – so royalties for February sales are paid at the end of March. KDP Print royalties are paid 60 days after the month of sale, so at the end of April for February sales.

The beauty of DIY self-publishing is that you have all of this information at your fingertips, 24 hours a day. This is vital for measuring the effectiveness of any social media or paid-for advertising campaigns you decide to run – and, of course, priceless for the satisfaction it offers as you see your story being shared with customers around the country or world!

You can view the snapshot image below in the resources folder at: selfpublishingadventures.com/resources using the password found in Chapter 29.

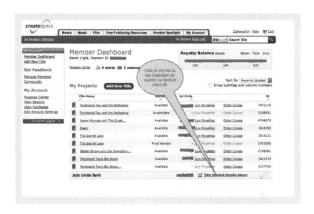

CreateSpace Royalty report snapshot – KDP Print has similar reports. View both full size in the resources folder.

Which Amazon stores will your book appear in?

The table overleaf shows which of Amazon's online stores around the world distribute CreateSpace/KDP Print books (meaning Amazon fulfils orders using its print on demand service).

Self-published Kindle titles (covered later) are made available in all stores below worldwide.

You will see minor differences between CreateSpace and KDP Print for Japan and Mexico. If these particular markets are important to you it will be worth checking the latest status on KDP Print. Logic says that everything will align once the move to KDP print is finalised. More generally, it will be worth checking for updates to all of this information on the KDP website as the available markets are likely to expand over time.

PRINT ON DEMAND DISTRIBUTION TO AMAZON STORES WORLDWIDE (JULY 2018)

Print on demand distribution to Amazon stores worldwide (July 2018)

Store	Country	CreateSpace	KDP Print
Amazon.com	USA	Yes	Yes
Amazon.co.uk	UK	Yes	Yes
Amazon.ca	Canada	Yes	Yes
Amazon.de	Germany	Yes	Yes
Amazon.fr	France	Yes	Yes
Amazon.es	Spain	Yes	Yes
Amazon.is	Italy	Yes	Yes
Amazon.nl	Holland	No	No
Amazon.mx	Mexico	Yes	Not yet*
Amazon.jp	Japan	No	Yes
Amazon.br	Brazil	No	No
Amazon.au	Australia	No	No
Amazon.in	India	No	No

*Wording on KDP's website July 2018. I'm assuming this means direct distribution is imminent here.

(eBooks are delivered in all stores.)

Note that where Amazon doesn't currently distribute in print, on some sites your book may show as available through third-party sellers who in turn would be supplied by Ingram Spark if you use them for wider distribution. See the section below for more on using Ingram Spark.

2. Ingram Spark – for non-Amazon distribution worldwide

In parallel with your Amazon distribution print strategy, when starting out I recommend using Ingram Spark to make your books available to order in bricks and mortar bookshops and non-Amazon online stores worldwide – even though Amazon also offers this wider distribution service (which they call 'Expanded Distribution') at the set-up stage.

Why Ingram Spark?

Ingram Spark, which offers a print on demand service very similar to Amazon's, is owned by the Ingram Group, a major worldwide book distributor whose electronic data feed goes out to tens of thousands of book retailers and wholesalers worldwide, enabling them to place orders quickly and easily. (It is this same data feed that CreateSpace/KDP Print uses if you choose Expanded Distribution at their set-up stage.) The wholesalers in turn feed this data into the book ordering services they use with the bricks and mortar and online bookshops they service.

You can view a list of Ingram Spark's Global Print distribution partners at *ingramspark.com/how-it-works/print-distribution-partners*

Why not use CreateSpace/KDP Print for all distribution?

- CreateSpace/KDP Print will be listed as the distributor of your title on the data feed. Since these are known to be Amazon companies, bookshops and online retailers may be less disposed to stock your title or (in the case of bricks and mortar shops) less inclined to order if they have to choose between different in-demand titles due to limited shelf-space or budget.

- They may also be less inclined to take your book on sale or return – known in the industry as 'on consignment' – if you walk in with copies to sell (they will need to look it up on their system for processing purposes and will see its provenance).

- CreateSpace/KDP Print will deduct 60% from your RRP on top of the fixed-price costs mentioned earlier, meaning lower royalties for you compared with your Amazon sales where they only deduct 40%. (In practice this means you are offering a 60% discount off the RRP.) CreateSpace/KDP Print require this extra 20% to allow them to offer a cut to the 'middleman' wholesaler who then sells your book on to the bookshops. However, as you will see below, with Ingram Spark you can choose what discount you want to offer this wider distribution network and so have more control over how much you will earn per sale.

Benefits of using Ingram Spark

- Ingram Book Company is listed as the distributor, so no risk of alienating bookshops.

- You get to choose what wholesale discount you want to offer retailers and wholesalers – from 30% or 35%, depending on the market, up to 55%. Note that the lower you go the less likely a bookshop will be to order your book as any discount much below 40% means they will earn very little from the sale. What's best for you will depend on your wider marketing strategy, but having the choice is a bonus and puts you in control of your profit per sale. See Chapter 11, page 129 for more on choosing your discount.

- Ingram Spark offers hard cover as an option, which may be of interest if you write picture books.

- Ingram Spark offers an efficient short print-run service, allowing you to order school and other event stock for delivery to home or elsewhere. *New June 2018: this now includes a* **personalisation** *option – search Ingram's site for more info.* Short-run orders from CreateSpace are not economical for non-US authors as they ship from the US (and CreateSpace is being phased out in any event). However, KDP Print's author copies are printed locally, albeit they are not offered for Australia, Holland or Brazil as I write. Assuming you are combining KDP Print and Ingram Spark, it will be worth comparing print and postage costs for school events and local bookshop stock when the time comes – and colour quality for picture books, as this can vary between the two.

How Ingram Spark works

The end-to-end process for upload and proofing through to final approval and 'on sale' is very similar to that of CreateSpace/KDP Print described above, with the following variations:

- There is a file set-up cost of $49 per title at the time of writing – however this is refunded if you place a single order of 50 or more books within 60 days of publication.
- The first revision with Ingram Spark is free – thereafter, at the time of writing, there is a charge of $25 for each revised file upload.*
- You need to choose what discount you want to offer to book wholesalers in the UK and worldwide. *(See 'Pricing your print book' in Chapter 11 for what to consider when setting your wholesale discounts – Ingram has online calculators to help you decide.)*
- You need to state whether or not you will allow returns of your unsold books by bookshops. *(I generally recommend saying no to returns, unless you are certain there is a large market for your book. I talk about this more in Chapter 23.)*

*__Tip__: if you're a member of the **Alliance of Independent Authors** (recommended – see Chapter 28), you may be eligible for a voucher code offering free set-up and free revisions over a set time. These offers come and go, so be sure to check. Certainly there is a code for 2018!

Ingram Spark sales reports – 'publisher compensation'

With Ingram Spark, as with CreateSpace/KDP Print, you have instant access to your sales and income reports (called 'publisher compensation reports') 24/7. You can run these for set or custom periods and by all or selected titles and/or countries. Payments are made 90 days in arrears. The only downside is you cannot see which wholesalers or online retailers within a given country ordered your books. (These reports are available by special request from Ingram's sister company, Lightning Source, which deals with larger publishers – but I'm not aware that you can request them with Ingram Spark.)

Why not use Ingram Spark to fulfil Amazon orders?

Since the Ingram feed goes out to Amazon as well as every other worldwide online retailer, you may be wondering why I don't recommend using Ingram Spark to fulfil Amazon's website orders.

This is perfectly possible but there are two downsides:

- You will often see 'Temporarily Out of Stock' messages posted on your Amazon sales page. This will be when Amazon hasn't ordered sufficient stock to keep up with orders, or – at launch – doesn't get in any stock until the first orders are placed. In contrast, Amazon's own print on demand books through CreateSpace/KDP Print will always show as 'In Stock'. I probably don't need to tell you how frustrating 'Out of Stock' messages can be on the world's biggest online book retailer during a launch, or a busy holiday period, when you want to drive customers to your Amazon page using social media or advertising!

- You only get indirect access to your sales reports – the Ingram Spark reports don't break down sales by channel as standard. This is a far cry from the daily instant reporting you get with CreateSpace/KDP Print – and not helpful for quickly adjusting targeted advertising on Amazon if you start to use this later down the line. *(See Chapter 24, 'Children's book advertising' for more on this topic.)*

To sum up, using KDP Print combined with Ingram Spark is what I would recommend when starting out with your print self-publishing (as CreateSpace is being phased out). When following this strategy I also recommend buying your own ISBN and using it on both platforms. I explain the reason for this in Chapter 9, which covers ISBNs in detail.

NB Ingram Spark didn't exist when I started out in 2011. As a result, I self-publish through their sister company, Lightning Source, which caters to small publishers. Both use the same print presses and distribution networks. The key difference is that Ingram Spark is set up to deal with individual (and beginner) authors, whereas Lightning Source isn't.

Alternatives to print on demand

Clearly, the beauty of using print on demand is that you don't need to hold any stock in order to sell your book online. At the same time, you can still order your own copies at cost for advance readers and reviewers, or for events or local bookshop supply.

However, for larger orders – typically of 100 or more books (and possibly less) – it may be cheaper to place short digital print runs with other printing firms instead of using Ingram Spark or CreateSpace/KDP Print. Being aware of this extra option is especially relevant for children's authors, as we often need large amounts of stock if visiting schools.

Below you'll find a list of short-run digital print companies in the UK that I've seen recommended by Alliance of Independent Authors members and in other forums – and I would certainly recommend investigating Clays who have an excellent reputation. Of course, you may find others close to where you live – and if you're outside the UK then it will be a case of researching online or in forums. In all cases I'd recommend getting testimonials from other authors if taking this route – both on the quality of service and the quality of the final book.

- Clays – **clays.co.uk**
- TJ International – **TJInternational.ltd.uk**
- CPI Print – **cpiprint.co.uk** (also offer full colour short-run)

A further reason (beyond cost) why you may wish to consider short print runs for larger orders is if you are actively looking to encourage bricks and mortar bookshops to stock your book. This is because, as a rule, bookshops don't tend to stock print on demand titles due to availability issues. I expand on this in Chapter 23 *'Getting your book into high street bookshops'*, where I also give detail on a service provided by Clays in the UK that offers a solution for self-published authors.

My own choice for school stock

The above all said, despite regularly ordering books in the hundreds I've mostly kept to ordering my school stock from my print on demand suppler and distributer, Lightning Source (Ingram Spark's sister company). Why? Because going with a separate company means new sets of files to prepare, new proofs to order and so on – and all of the associated time. As an indie author I have enough plates to spin without complicating my life further! In short, I've mostly stuck with print on demand for simplicity – but that was a personal choice and I'm not suggesting it is always the right one. There was just one exception in the early days with one of my picture books where I placed a short up-front run due to the silk finish of paper I needed. I cover this at the end of the section *'DIY Interior layout: picture books'* on page 98.

If you're more organised than I am – and are confident that you will sell or find a home for the books you order – then short digital runs may well be right for you as a cost saving choice.

6

FILES NEEDED TO CREATE YOUR PRINT BOOK

Whether you choose print on demand or short digital print runs, the two key files needed in order to create your book are:

- a print-ready cover PDF file (made up left to right of back, spine and front cover)
- a print-ready interior PDF file – this is an exact replica of your book's interior content and layout

'Print-ready' PDFs are much larger in size than a standard PDF file and include complexities such as 'embedded fonts', 'flattened image layers' and certain colour settings that are still a bit of a mystery to me, beyond knowing the terms! To create them you need specialist software, such as Adobe Acrobat Pro, Photoshop or InDesign. Simply choosing 'save as PDF' using the standard program on your Mac or PC won't do the trick.

Creating a print-ready book cover file

Any illustrator you work with will know how to prepare a print-ready book cover file. All you need to do is provide them with links to the templates and file specifications they need for Amazon and Ingram Spark. (There are slight variations for each platform, meaning that separate cover PDFs are required for each.)

Resources and links

The links below (which you'll also find in the resources folder) are correct at the time of writing – otherwise search for 'cover templates' or 'cover file submission guidelines' on the relevant website.

- **CreateSpace cover file templates**
  createspace.com/Help/Book/Artwork.do

- **KDP Print cover file templates**
  kdp.amazon.com/en_US/cover-templates

- **Ingram Spark cover file templates and submission guidelines**
  myaccount.ingramspark.com/Portal/Tools/
  CoverTemplateGenerator

Should you create your own cover?

I would not recommend trying to do your own cover artwork, unless you are an illustrator **and** expert at layout. To read more about finding and working with a cover designer – or sourcing pre-made children's book covers, see Chapter 7, *'Print book design – planning and resources'.*

Creating a print-ready interior file

There are three key options for creating your print-ready interior PDF:

- Use one of CreateSpace / KDP Print's free interior Word templates* to do the layout yourself then either pay a freelancer to do the conversion to print-ready PDF for you or convert it yourself using Adobe Acrobat Pro DC (requires a subscription).

- Outsource the whole of layout and file conversion to a freelancer – you simply provide an A4 Word document, any design instructions and interior images. They will know where to get the templates for your book's size or will have their own.

- Use paid-for 'pre-designed' templates and tools to lay out and convert your interior.

Ingram Spark doesn't provide interior templates at the time of writing, however the PDF files you create using CreateSpace/KDP Print's interior templates work fine for Ingram Spark assuming you are using the same book size there (and you should be!).

Should you lay out your interior yourself?

If there are no images inside your children's book (typically, a middle grade novel), then it's perfectly possible for you to do the layout using the free templates provided by

CreateSpace/KDP Print – it's easy to adapt these to your style needs. When it comes to illustrated chapter books and picture books there's a lot more to think about, but it's by no means impossible.

I discuss all of the above, as well as the pros and cons of using paid-for pre-designed children's book interior templates and other formatting tools, in the next chapter: *'Print book design – planning and resources'.*

RESOURCES AND LINKS

- **CreateSpace interior templates**
  createspace.com/Products/Book/InteriorPDF.jsp

- **KDP Print interior templates**
  kdp.amazon.com/en_US/help/topic/G201834230

- **Adobe Acrobat Pro DC pricing info** – search 'Adobe Acrobat plans' to find the pricing page for your country.

- **Freelance formatters and layout artists** – see the resources list at the end of the next chapter.

(These are also in the online resources folder.)

7

PRINT BOOK DESIGN: PLANNING AND RESOURCES

This section covers:

- Finding and working with an illustrator
- Ready-made children's book covers
- Finding and working with an interior layout artist
- DIY interior: layout tips for chapter books or middle grade novels
- DIY interior: layout tips for picture books
- Pre-designed interior children's book templates
- Specialist tools for children's picture books

Finding and working with an illustrator

There are lots of places to find illustrators online – and a wide range of budgets to choose from. The list overleaf is by no means exhaustive. And don't forget to ask fellow children's authors for their own recommendations.

At the end of the day the choice is very personal. However, you will clearly be looking for someone whose style you like and fits with what you can see is popular with your target age group/genre. 'Different' is fine too – but it will need to stand out as both brilliant and appropriate for your target audience, and that can be very subjective!

WEBSITES WHERE YOU CAN SEARCH FOR ILLUSTRATORS

- SCBWI.org (The Society for Children's Book Writers and Illustrators)
- Upworks.com
- Fiverr.com
- ChildrensIlustrators.com
- Behance.net
- 99designs.co.uk
- Guru.com
- *LinkedIn or Facebook* – *children's books illustrator groups*

Get samples and testimonials

This goes without saying. The methods for listing your project, obtaining samples and testimonials and agreeing a price will differ on each website. Some initial samples you may have to pay for, in other cases you may not – it will depend on the illustrator.

When comparing illustrators that you like on the freelance sites, look beyond overall satisfaction rates for the quality of the end design. Consider feedback on timing, reliability, ease of contact and how easy they are to work with – either by studying the star ratings and comments on these aspects or by contacting previous customers to ask. Also look at repeat hire rate and project completion rate. If an illustrator you like on a freelancer site shows a low repeat hire rate but has been around for a while, I'd be asking why – ditto if his or her project completion rate is low compared with the average.

This is all much easier when considering illustrators used by people you know!

Costs and payment

Rates for illustrations vary widely – especially in this global market – so you will need to compare the market and decide what works for your budget.

Your payment options are either per hour or per illustration (with the number of revisions per illustration agreed in advance). Most writers pay per illustration because this means you know your budget up front – thus your project will consist of set number of illustrations for a set price. Hourly rates might range from $10 - $35 and per illustration from around $25 and upwards. These really are ballpark figures! They will vary by the illustrator's location, working method and experience so go online and see what's right for you.

On the freelancer sites you can usually opt to pay either on completion of each illustration or at certain milestones, such as at certain percentage completion points during the project. How you choose to do this is up for negotiation and will depend on how many illustrations you need and how soon. Clearly, setting milestones will (hopefully) encourage faster turnarounds. You also have the option to add bonuses if you wish – again, if you have a tight deadline this can be useful to encourage the illustrator to prioritise your work.

What about royalty split?

I think it highly unlikely that any illustrator would agree royalty share (ie providing illustrations in return for a percentage of your income from book sales). It would require too much up-front risk and unpaid time commitment for them. On that basis I personally wouldn't ask about this as it could prove awkward and get things off to the wrong start if you really want to work with that person.

Copyright

To prevent any future arguments about use of the artwork, you need to put in place a contract that transfers copyright ownership of the illustrations to you upon payment. The wording for this needn't be complicated, and most of the freelancer websites have this built into the overarching terms of service that everyone signs up to.

What follows is a simple form of words that you could use or adapt if not using a freelance site that covers this already. However, please bear in mind that **I am not a lawyer and this may have a UK bias**, so please have it checked if you have any concerns. I can't personally guarantee that this will cover your situation!

If an illustrator isn't happy to sign over copyright you must respect this and either come to a different agreement (beyond the scope of this book) or look elsewhere.

COPYRIGHT TRANSFER EXAMPLE FORM OF WORDS

The Illustrator acknowledges and agrees that all Work undertaken for the Author is "work for hire" and that upon receipt of full payment for the Work from the Author (such amount to be agreed between the Author and the Illustrator from time to time), the Work shall become the sole and exclusive property of the Author. The Illustrator also acknowledges and agrees that, upon receipt of full payment for the Work, the Illustrator automatically and irrevocably assigns to the Author all right, title and interest in and to the Intellectual Property Rights held by the Illustrator. The Illustrator further confirms and acknowledges that, for the avoidance of doubt, upon receipt of payment for the Work and the Author thereby becoming the copyright owner of the Work, the Author shall hold the exclusive worldwide rights to publish and sell the Work in any form whatsoever at the Author's sole discretion under its own name and/or under other imprints or trade names.

The Illustrator may at any time request consent from the Author to use the Work for his or her own marketing purposes, including without limitation in the Illustrator's portfolio or on his or her website. The Author shall not unreasonably withhold consent to any such request by the Illustrator.

DEFINITIONS:

Author *means [name of author].*

Illustrator *means [name of illustrator].*

Intellectual Property Rights *means all copyright, database rights, all rights in any trade marks, designs or patents, and all other intellectual property rights and equivalent or similar forms of protection existing anywhere in the world in, or arising out of or directly in connection with, the Work.*

Work *means all sketches and illustrations, whether fully or partially completed, together with any associated digital files, created by the Illustrator for the Author pursuant to any agreement, correspondence or other form of engagement entered into or made between the Author and the Illustrator from time to time, as the case may be.*

Cover design – tips for briefing your illustrator

To help your illustrator come up with a design that you'll be happy with, do lots of research in advance, and give as much information as possible to steer them in the right direction. This will help minimise misunderstandings and endless rounds of revisions.

RESEARCH CHECKLIST:

- Look at other cover designs in your target age group for stories of a similar genre. Your aim is to come up with something that fits in with the other designs (look and feel) while still having its own identity. In short, your book needs to sit happily on the virtual or real shelf alongside those other books.

- Visit bookshops / libraries and look online at Amazon and other online stores for your research.

- Pay attention to colours, font style and size (titles / author names), spines, and back cover layout and content – are there ideas that you particularly like and could ask your illustrator to mimic or adapt?

- **Look at the designs in thumbnail size** – this is crucial. Which stand out on your desktop, phone or tablet? And why? Is it easy to read the book's title and the author's name in thumbnail size? Which don't grab your attention and why?

- **Think about visual narrative** – you want the illustration of your front cover to give an 'at-a-glance' snapshot of the 'story' within. This may be in the form of a scene from the book – or achieved through some sort of collage of characters / images. How are other authors achieving this with their book covers?

- Pick examples of the books you like and include these with your illustrator's brief together with notes to say what you like about them.

- If you have an image in your mind's eye for your front cover that you're finding hard to describe – whether of the main illustration or some element of it – are there any photos you could find online to make your brief clearer?

Tip: A quick Google search often helps at the briefing stage. For example, when briefing the cover illustration for *Henry Haynes and the Great Escape* I had a clear idea in my mind of how I wanted the gorilla cage setting to look, based on memories from trips to London Zoo with my children – but my sketches were next to useless! So, I googled London Zoo and found a few images and took screenshots.

I've also used this method to find a photo with a 'look' or expression of a certain character that I have in my mind. For example, when briefing the character of Walter for *Walter Brown and the Magician's Hat* front cover, I searched through faces in children's clothes catalogues and junior football club websites until I found something that clicked. This gave my illustrator a head start on coming up with a look that I would like.

(I couldn't ask him to read the whole book to form his own view of the character – English isn't his first language and he's extremely busy anyway!)

Front cover tells the story. The cage image was based on a Google search.

Ready-made children's book covers

Yes, these do exist! The basic set-up is that you buy the ready-designed cover and the site offering the service will add your book title, any subtitle and author name plus the back-cover blurb – then create the eBook and print book cover versions for you, ready for upload.

This way of working lends itself much better to adult genre books in my view – where the same thriller or sci-fi cover can often be a suitable fit for more than one story. I don't think it works easily for children's books. However, if you're struggling for a story idea, a pre-designed children's book cover may give you the inspiration you're looking for.

I've not used any of the sites below, so cannot vouch for them. However, they seem to have good children's book collections that may offer inspiration. Be sure to read the small print around payment and copyright if you're thinking of using one of these sites – and try to get testimonials from other authors who've used them.

PRE-MADE BOOK COVER WEBSITES

- **Bookcoverzone.com**
- **Boocover4u.com**
- **Thebookcoverdesigner.com**

Finding and working with an interior layout artist

It is perfectly possible to prepare your children's book interior yourself, using free or paid-for tools, and I cover this in the next two sections. However, if the thought of this fills you with dread – or if you're looking for a highly quirky or styled interior – there are plenty of freelancers available who will design the layout for you then create your print-ready file.

RECOMMENDED PLACES TO START YOUR SEARCH

Reedsy.com (Remember: if you sign up using my affiliate link at **reedsy.com/a/inglis** you'll get a $20 credit towards your first project.)

Alliance of Independent Authors Self-Publishing Services Directory (bit.ly / ALLiDirectory) To benefit from the partner member discounts I'd recommend joining ALLi. See Chapter 28 for more information on the benefits of joining and how to sign up.

lawstondesign.com – Rachel Lawston, who designed the cover for this book, is a partner member of the Alliance of Independent Authors and offers a generous discount off her fees for indie authors who are members. She has worked for the traditional publishers for many years and designed the iconic black and white cover for Malorie Blackman's *Noughts & Crosses* – as well as covers for Matt Haig. Need I say more?

Lighthouse24.com – I used Doug Heatherly at Lighthouse24 in Texas for all my print books in the early days before Vellum (covered on page 84) and still use him as my first port of call if I get stuck. He has been formatting books for CreateSpace and Ingram Spark for years and offers a dependable service for straightforward layouts.

DIY interior layout: chapter books and middle grade novels

If you're writing a chapter book or middle grade novel and are confident using basic packages such as Word, it is possible (with a bit of planning) to prepare the interior of your book yourself using the CreateSpace/KDP Print templates listed earlier. You then either create the print-ready PDF from the file or ask someone else to do this for you.

Here are the key things you'll need to think about:

- Paper colour and size
- Font choice
- Font size
- Line spacing
- Ragged right or justified text?
- Paragraph design
- Frequency and placement of illustrations
- Chapter heading design

Paper colour and size

Most readers have probably never noticed this, but it's the norm in the book industry for fiction (both adult and children's fiction) to use cream/off-white paper. Notable exceptions that use white paper are most picture books and the occasional middle grade title or series, such as the Goth Girl books by Chris Riddle. Most non-fiction books use white paper.

Your paper size is, of course, your book's size and you will decide on this after researching the market, as described earlier.

Most children's fiction uses size 5 x 8 inches (203 x 127 mm). For my books I went with 5.25 x 8 inches (203 x 133 mm) – I honestly can't remember why – but it is almost the same and sits comfortably alongside other chapter books and middle grade fiction in bookshops. The Word templates provided by CreateSpace/KDP Print include these and other sizes.

Tip: Not all paper sizes are available in cream on both CreateSpace/KDP Print and Ingram Spark, so check this at the outset when choosing. Having to use different paper sizes to achieve cream paper on both platforms would require two lots of interior files, two cover files and separate ISBNs due to the different book sizes – this would be both costly and confusing and you clearly don't want to go down this route!

(See Chapter 9 for an explanation of ISBNs.)

Fonts, line spacing and paragraph style

As with most tasks, your best starting point is to take a look at books similar to yours (target age group and genre) and make a note of their styles.

What you'll find is that the font choice will often reflect the 'character' of the book. With *The Secret Lake*, for example, I knew I wanted the font to feel classic (in line with the story), yet not be too 'heavy going' and old-fashioned.

The Secret Lake interior

Here's what I settled on after a lot of looking around and experimentation:

- **Book Antiqua** for the body text, because it is light and clean, but also feels 'traditional'.
- **Point size 11**, because 12 looked *just* too large (and potentially 'babyish') for the 8-11-year-old market.
- **Line spacing of 1.2**, because single-line spacing looked too cramped, and anything wider began to suggest the feel of a chapter book.
- **Justified text,** because ragged text felt too 'young' for my target audience.
- **No drop caps at chapter start** – I wanted to keep it simple (though admittedly Vellum software, explained on page 84, didn't exist then, so perhaps I will change my mind in the future if I play around with the style!)
- **Paragraph indentation 4mm** – I tried deeper but it looked awkward to my eye and other middle grade books I looked at seemed to use this.

I worked all of this out after poring over similar books in the library and from my children's bookshelf at home, then printing off different samples from my story, formatted in my planned 5.25 x 8 book size, to give me a true feel for the reader's experience.

6 - The Boy Thief

'Oh well now, how exciting! Do come and have a cool drink with us!' said Miss Walker. At the mention of fluid Tom perked up again. 'I'm sure the girls would love to hear all about Australia. Do you have a governess over there?' They all trooped out onto the lawn.

'A governess? Oh, yes!' Stella fixed another glare on Tom. Tom, his thoughts focused on cold juice, nodded solemnly.

As they all helped Miss Walker move the rug and a pile of leather bound books into the shade of a tree, Stella found herself glancing at the row of houses on the far side of the lawn.

'Is there something wrong?' said Sophie suddenly.

'Hey, there's our house!' shouted Tom, pointing.

'What are you talking about?' said Sophie. 'That's *our* house!'

Stella laughed and quickly shook her head. 'Don't be silly, Tom. Our house is in Australia!' She then clenched

25

The Secret Lake sample

Eeek! The Runaway Alien interior

With *Eeek! The Runaway Alien* I was going for a different feel altogether. This is a fun and fast-paced chapter book for ages 7-10 and very much aimed at reluctant readers.

How the text looked on the page was critical for (hopefully) getting readers to keep turning the pages.

Here's what I settled on for *Eeek!*:

- **Georgia, font** – the rounded design feels easy on the eye and 'inviting'
- **Point size 12** – helps the text look easy to get through.
- **Line-spacing 1.2** – again, easy on the eye and felt right when tested on the page.
- **Justified text** – ragged looked and felt a little too 'young' for a core readership 7-10

- Our postman with a parcel
- The National Lottery man to say we'd won (dream on!)

or

- Mum, hot and sweaty after the gym, having forgotten her key as usual.

In fact it was none of these. Standing at our door that Saturday morning was, I'm not kidding you, an *alien!*

Now, most people would jump out of their skins at the sight on their doorstep of a bald-headed fluorescent green monster with pale blue smoke wafting from its tiny semicircular ears. But there was something about this alien that touched my heart. Whether it was his large slow-blinking pink-red eyes, his snub nose, his friendly smile, or simply the fact that he was exactly my height, I

2

Eeek! The Runaway Alien sample

Henry Haynes and the Great Escape interior

As *Henry Haynes and the Great Escape* is aimed at a starter reader (ages 6-8) I went for Georgia point size 12 with much wider line spacing (double) and ragged right rather than justified text, as seen opposite.

Again, this was after studying the style of similar books and printing off pages to scale.

Henry's first thought was to run from the room. But curiosity quickly overtook his fear and as he now poked his nose down into the hole he could see a mass of letters whirling about in what looked like a deep dark cooking pot.

His pillow, which should have been underneath the book, seemed to have vanished,

15

Henry Haynes and the Great Escape sample

Chapter headings

Whether you keep these simple or add graphics will, again, depend on your genre and target age group. If keeping it simple you can, of course, add expression through your chapter font choice, which doesn't need to match the body copy font. Here's what I did on three of my books:

- With *The Secret Lake* I felt that the chapter titles were themselves sufficient to add a sense of mystery and encourage readers to keep going – so I simply picked a font that complemented the style of the body. This is a common approach for most middle grade novels.

- With *Eeek!* I didn't want chapter titles – the diary format didn't lend itself to this and I'd seen other similar books that worked well with the 'One' 'Two' 'Three' etc as chapter headings. However, to make the reading experience more interesting, I decided to add in a wisp of smoke above each chapter number, to echo the smoke that comes out of Eeek's ears. This light touch added a sense of fun that I felt would amuse all of my readers – and help more reluctant readers keep on going!

- With *Walter Brown and the Magician's Hat* the story somehow demanded additional fizz, despite the chapter names. As you will see, I settled for a simple burst of magical stars, which – as with Eeek's smoke wisps – were quick for my illustrator to design.

One

It was a fairly typical Saturday morning in our house. Dad was in the garden emptying out the shed (again!). Mum had gone to the gym for her early morning workout. Rory (my four-year-old brother) was on the sofa wearing Dad's snorkel and mask watching his favourite underwater scene in 'Finding Nemo'. I was scoring goals against the kitchen wall in front of an imaginary crowd of 50,000.

That's when the doorbell rang.

Eeek! chapter header with smoke wisp

1 – The Birthday Surprise

As dawn broke on the morning of Walter Brown's tenth birthday he hadn't the faintest idea that his life was about to change forever. Like most other boys his age he was still fast asleep in bed.

Walter Brown chapter header with magic dust

Of course, you can make your chapter designs far more sophisticated if you want to. Do your research, then decide what's best for your book.

Frequency and placement of images

There are a number of ways to plan for images in chapter books or illustrated books for older readers. For example, you may decide that you want X number of illustrations per chapter, or one on every other page – or simply randomly based on your gut feel as the story progresses.

I'm not aware of any hard and fast rules on this, but I went with gut feel when planning the illustrations for *Henry Haynes and the Great Escape, Eeek! The Runaway Alien* and *Walter Brown and the Magician's Hat* – albeit keeping in mind the frequency of illustrations in books aimed at a similar audience. Below is the method I used – though you may find a better way, of course.

- Once the story was complete and out for editing, I skim-read it in one sitting, pausing to mark where I felt an image would work well – or where I had had a particularly strong image in my head at the time of writing. This first step, which you can do on-screen or using a print-out, identified the core images for me and enabled me to start briefing my illustrator. I knew these images would be used.

- After the editing stage – when I knew the text wouldn't change – I flowed the story into the

CreateSpace template for the book's size, taking care to use my chosen font size, correct line spacing and so on – and from there was able to mark where my core images would appear using placeholder frames in the desired image size. Doing this enabled me to see the effect on page-flow. Sometimes I couldn't place the image frame exactly where I wanted to, due to page-ends, but there was nothing that significantly impacted the reader experience.

- Next, by viewing the document at 10% or 25% on my screen, I could quickly see where any unacceptable imbalances lay, or more images were needed. Mindful of budget, I often kept these extras quite simple – for example zooming in on a detail that was mentioned in the text – such as *Eeek!* spinning the globe in his hand (see the image overleaf). These unplanned extras provided the extra visual relief I felt was needed to keep the more reluctant young readers turning the pages.

- As above, I added placeholder frames for the new extra images and reflowed the document from there.

Small image used at final edit to break up text

I strongly believe in putting yourself in the reader's shoes, and the second phase of adding further images once the book was flowed into its template was, for me, key to giving my more reluctant readers the best possible experience.

There may well be better formulas out there used by traditional publishers for planning illustrations. If you know of them, give them a go!

Image quality, inserting and resizing your images

Be aware of these crucial rules for preparing and inserting images:

- Your black and white images should have a minimum print resolution of 230 dpi (dots per inch) – and ideally 300 dpi – to avoid error messages at upload of the print-ready PDF to CreateSpace/KDP

Print/Ingram Spark. Any lower and the image could appear pixelated (fuzzy) on the printed page. Your illustrator will know this but it's worth checking and discussing at the briefing stage.

- Size is crucial too. If the artwork comes back smaller than the finished size you need, it will lose image quality when you enlarge it, and if it's way too large you risk losing detail when reducing the size. So, at the briefing stage be sure to tell the illustrator the page size and image size you are aiming for – including image shape, such as square or rectangular, if that is critical. *(The illustrator is likely to make the image larger than you need but in the correct proportions. The percentage increase over and above the actual image size you need that won't lose detail when reduced will depend on the style of the illustration and what medium they work in – a good illustrator will know and understand this so you shouldn't run into problems if you briefed them on the size you need at the outset.)*

- When inserting the images into your Word interior template always use the **Insert > Image** function – do not use copy and paste as this downsizes the image quality and will lead to rejection.

- If you need to resize the image after you've inserted it, do this outside of Word using the **Tools > image > resize / Tools > adjust size** command (on a Mac) and equivalent on a PC then insert it again. Don't resize it within the document and don't just drag it to make it smaller as, again, this can lead to quality issues. (As I write, I have a feeling you may, in fact, get away with *reducing* the size of a black and white illustration within the document, but don't hold me to it!)

Using Vellum software for interior layout (Mac only)

If you work on a Mac I have some great news for you. There is a wonderful piece of software called Vellum, which has revolutionised book formatting for Mac users in the last few years.

Initially it catered only for eBooks, but in late 2016 it introduced print book formatting. The book you are reading now is formatted with Vellum.

In relation to children's books, I can't sing Vellum's praises highly enough for eBook formatting (including those with black and white or even colour pictures), and I cover this in more detail in Chapter 8.

For print books it fares a little less well at the time of writing due to a fairly narrow range of fonts, font sizes and line spacing options. However, it still works well for middle grade novels and upwards. Vellum's owners are aware and have logged requests to introduce additional choices that would work for early reader chapter books and indeed picture books – but I have no idea where in the development queue these requests are sitting.

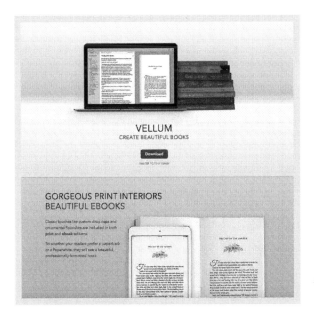

Vellum – formats for print and eBook (Mac only)

Advantages of using Vellum

- A beautifully simple interface – making it easy to upload both text and images and create the different components of your book.
- Automatic warnings where images aren't optimised for print (or screen) – with a quick and easy way to replace them with the correct size.
- Allows you to create an eBook version at the same time (covered later).
- Quick and easy to test and switch between different styles, instantly showing how your book will look. Key text elements styles to choose from include: body text font and size; line spacing; chapter header; opening chapter first line – including drop caps

options; block quotes style; verse style; ornamental break style – including the option to upload your own image.

- Offers a range of styles for images, including captions and border types and a full-page image option.
- Allows for text flow around smaller sized images.
- Easy to find and easy to follow help notes should you need them.
- Polite and responsive email help *(direct from owners at the time of writing)* if you really get stuck.
- Quick and easy to format a middle grade novel – with or without illustrations.
- **Free to try out – see below.**

The best bit is that **you can download and try Vellum for free** – and indeed create a whole book. You would only need to sign up at the point you wish to publish your book.

Limitations of using Vellum

- Only works on a Mac – at the time of writing there are no imminent plans for this to change.
- The limited choice of fonts, font sizes and line spacing makes it unsuitable for early readers and picture books where larger fonts and much wider line spacing is required – currently these are on the wish list, but with no indication of timeline.
- A limited choice of book sizes at the time of writing – but the industry standards are all there.

- Limited flexibility to customise chapter headings (eg starting position on page and accompanying image position/size) – but by no means a deal breaker.

Previous limitations around title page and back-matter design (owing to working within a template environment) have been largely resolved with the introduction of a full-page image element. This means you can design these pages elsewhere using free or paid-for tools then bring them in as a full-page image as a workaround.

My most recent edition of my illustrated lower middle grade novel *Walter Brown and the Magician's Hat* was formatted for print with Vellum and the only limitation I found was font choice. The one I went with was 'Crimson Text' – but I'd have preferred something with a little more presence. (I doubt the children notice though!) I was able to customise everything else to my satisfaction, including the images at the start of each chapter.

Vellum cost

The one-off cost at the time of writing is:

- $199 to create unlimited eBooks for life
- $249.99 to create unlimited eBooks and paperbacks for life

Software upgrades are regular and free.

Find out more at **bit.ly/VellumKaren** *(Disclosure: this is an affiliate link. I'll earn a referral commission at no extra cost to you if you go on to buy Vellum.)* Otherwise go to **Vellum.pub**

Ready-made interior templates: chapter books or middle grade novels

Joel Friedlander – based in the US – has been blogging about self-publishing since before I started my journey and is very well respected in the industry. He certainly knows his stuff when it comes to print. A few years ago, he launched a book design template website that includes children's book interiors – see screenshot below.

Children's book templates – one of several choices from bookdesigntemplates.com

If you don't want to DIY and you don't want to hire a freelance layout artist, this could be another option. The templates come with detailed instructions which, at the time of writing, you can access before buying. Take a look at these to get a feel for how easy you would find them to follow. There is also a US-based help desk. I would also recommend asking for testimonials from other children's authors. What is certain is that the final product will work and will look good.

The cost at the time of writing is $59 for a single book licence, for which you can create both a print and eBook, and $112 for a licence for multiple titles use. The templates come in print book trim sizes of 5.06 x 7.81", 5 x 8" and 6 x 9".

Find out more at **bookdesigntemplates.com**

After hunting around, this is the only 'ready-made' interior children's book templates site that I can recommend looking into. If you've found other quality ones, do let me know.

DIY Interior layout: picture books

Unless you are an illustrator or have a strong eye for design and know how to use layout packages such as InDesign, I would only recommend trying to design your picture book interior yourself if you plan to keep the layout extremely simple. By 'simple' I mean text above and/or below one or two images centred on each page, or a double page spread with text on one side and the illustration on the opposite page.

This is the route I took with my first two picture books *Ferdinand Fox's Big Sleep* and *Ferdinand Fox and the Hedgehog* due to budget constraints and not having an eye or the technical expertise for complex design. Had I engaged a layout artist I know these stories could look a lot more fun and innovative. However, picture book sales for me have until recently been hard to scale and this meant that I couldn't justify the cost of a layout artist on top of the illustration costs. As my picture books have started to sell in higher numbers online this is something I'm considering for the future though.

The rest of this section talks about how to plan and create a simple layout for a colour picture book using Word.

Paper colour and size

Make sure you choose a paper size that's available through both CreateSpace/KDP Print and Ingram Spark, assuming you're using print on demand. This is easy to check by looking at their cover and interior paper size templates. As already mentioned, most colour picture books use white paper and I'm assuming you'll be going with this too.

Picture book page and word count

Most picture books are 32 pages and 500-1,000 words long. (Word count can of course vary from very few right up to 1,000, but the golden rule is generally fewer is better.) The second most common page count is 24 pages. If these lengths don't suit your story, then any multiple of four will work – but bear in mind that 24- and 32-page books are tried and tested and will sit comfortably alongside the competition in bookshops if you're hoping to persuade booksellers to take yours.

For planning purposes, these page count numbers *exclude* the back and front cover (and the insides of each of these which are made from the same sheet) but need to *include ex*tra pages such as title page, dedication and so on – this is important to understand when mapping out your story as it means you probably have only 24-28 pages to play with for a 32-page picture book, depending on how you want to use your front and back matter pages. (I got this wrong first time around!)

Note that for printing purposes your page count needs to be divisible by four. If you vary from this the printer will add blank pages at the end.

Picture book storyboarding

This is working out on one piece of paper how your story – the pictures and the words – will flow through the book. A storyboard is an essential first planning step before going on to make up a full-size dummy. It gives you a birds' eye view of where your text and illustrations will sit and makes it easy to see what is and isn't working.

Because you are working at a high level it's also relatively quick to make changes, using revised storyboards if necessary. This is much more sensible than to trying to work with a full mock-up at the outset, no matter how sure you think you are of your story flow. (I made this mistake with my first picture book *Ferdinand Fox's Big Sleep* and wasted a lot of time as a result!)

See overleaf for a simple example of a 32-page picture book storyboard that I put together, along with the download link.

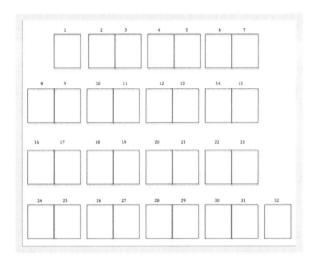

32-page picture book storyboard

You can find any number of downloadable templates by searching on Google. Or you can download my above 32-page colour picture book storyboard template at **www.bit.ly/kareninglisstoryboard**

Practical tips for storyboarding your children's picture book

These tips are based on my personal experience. I am not an illustrator, but I briefed my artist quite closely on all required pictures as I had a strong sense of what I wanted – we work well together this way.

TIP 1: BEFORE STARTING, TAKE A LOOK AT THE COMPETITION

I borrowed a lot of picture books from the local library and rummaged around in the loft for old favourites we've kept, such as *Hairy Maclary.* I was interested to study not just how the publishers had placed and interwoven the text and illustrations, but also to see how they had used their front and back matter pages (title page, half title, about the author etc).

What's acceptable, such as inclusion of illustrations in with copyright information, and the sequence in which the title page appears seems to be pretty flexible. I have a fun double page collage spread at the start of *Ferdinand Fox's Big Sleep* – it features a lot of the food we later see Ferdinand dreaming about, offering additional discussion and learning opportunities. I got the idea for this from some of the books I looked at.

Tip 2: Be ready to compromise

Ferdinand Fox's Big Sleep is 436 words long and made up of 13 sets of four-line rhyming verse. I had a reasonably clear idea of what pictures would go with which text as they had always played naturally in my head. However, because I wanted to make my book fit the traditional 32-page model, when I came to do the storyboard I had to cut planned pictures in some places (no room) and include unplanned pictures in other places (to avoid a text-only page).

I also had to change my 'master plan'! I had initially envisaged text on the left-hand page and an image on the right-hand page throughout – as with *Hairy Maclary*. However, it soon became clear that this wouldn't work all the way through – not just because of page-count restrictions, but also because the varying pace of the story demanded more frequent pictures in some places than in others. Having the high-level storyboard was a must for solving these challenges.

TIP 3: PUT YOURSELF IN THE READER'S SHOES

To ensure that you end up with an engaging spread of images and words, put yourself in the reader's shoes (parent/adult and child) and constantly ask yourself:

- 'Is the variety and mix of illustrations/words from one page to the next sufficient to keep readers – and watchers – engaged?'
- 'Do all pages offer opportunities for questions, discussion, thought, laughter, pointing and/or learning?'
- 'Is the story progressing at an acceptable pace visually and/or through the words?' (*This doesn't mean it needs to be a fast pace, of course – that will depend on the story.*)

We all know which books we read to our children that we enjoyed and returned to again and again – and I can certainly remember some that I found boring! Keep these common-sense questions in mind when planning your storyboard. They will help you know when it's right.

TIP 4: MAKE USE OF COLOUR CODING

On a first run with your storyboard, perhaps use a coloured cross or blob to indicate where you feel that an illustration is needed – be that on the same page as the text or on a facing page. You could also vary the size of your blobs or crosses to indicate the nature and size of each illustration (small, medium, large, close-up shot/full scene etc). I am no artist, but I certainly found this approach came naturally and gave me an immediate sense of the book's visual balance.

Once you're happy that the mix feels right, and that the text will fit, create a second version where you either sketch the image crudely, or (if, like me, you're not an illustrator) use colour text to describe the image needed.

The example below, which uses colour text instead of sketches, can be viewed in full size and focus in the resources folder at *selfpublishingadventures.com/resources* – see Chapter 29 for the password.

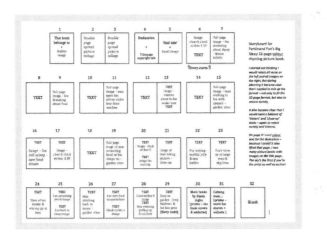

View full size in the resources folder.

Creating a mock-up

Once you are 99% certain that your story is mapped correctly, create a full-size mock-up of your book. This will enable you to leaf through and get the real 'reader experience'. It also gives you the chance to be absolutely sure that the pace of the story and mix of illustrations feels right. If it doesn't, you may need to return to your storyboard – or you may be able to make minor adjustments on your mock-up.

Follow the 10-step process below to create your mock-up:

This example assumes a 32-page picture book, but it can be adjusted for any page number.

1. Divide your book's page count by four and add one: for a 32-page picture book this comes to nine (8 +1).
2. Cut out nine pages of blank paper measuring double your book's page dimensions – eg if your book is 8 x 10 inches, cut out nine sheets of paper measuring 16 x 20 inches.
3. Lay the paper flat in a pile in the correct orientation then fold over in half from left to right or vice versa (in one batch) down the middle.
4. Press the fold flat then secure the fold line vertically with a loose rubber band or string or staple it from the outside.
5. To avoid any confusion, mark the outer wrap-around page as 'cover' at the front and the back, inside and out (or you could use a different colour paper for it).
6. Write in 'copyright page' 'title page' etc on the first few front matter pages, based on your storyboard.
7. Print out your story text on A4 paper, separated into sections. Use the font style, font size and line spacing from your research. Format any paragraphs in line

with your envisaged layout on each page. *(Remember: if something doesn't work as planned you can come back and change this.)*

8. Cut out the text for each page. Position, adjust and glue in place with placeholder frames/sketches for your planned images, as close to scale as you can.

9. Add notes for the back-matter pages from your storyboard – or print off and glue in the full information to scale if you've already drafted it, eg 'About the Author' text.

10. Read through, ponder, share with beta readers, and get feedback. If there are major issues with the flow or image choices, go back to your text and storyboard and re-plan from there. Otherwise make any minor adjustments to the dummy – then get ready to create your first proof .

Tip: Once you have your image files you could repeat this process and add the real images to size – and/or mock up a dummy on-screen in Word, then reduce the view to 10% to give you the same birds' eye view as the storyboard. I did this as a final step before sending my text file and images for *Ferdinand Fox's Big Sleep* to my formatter to lay out for me.

Picture book next steps

Once you've finalised your layout and added the words and images into your Word interior file template you can either hand over the document to an experienced formatter to check and create your print-ready PDF (this is what I do – recommended unless you are tech savvy) or convert it yourself if you have Adobe Acrobat and are confident that your images have been inserted and sized correctly without compromising the print resolution.

A final note on paper finish for picture books

Most traditionally published picture books use silk finish paper, which is slightly thicker and more 'sticky-finger-proof' than standard paper. Unfortunately, this finish isn't available through print on demand, so if you're dead set on it you'll need to go the short digital print run route. This will require up-front orders in the several hundred to make any financial sense (colour printing doesn't come cheap) so I would only recommend this approach if (a) you're actively looking to stock your book in lots of bookshops – which will be an uphill struggle without the support of a national marketing team **and** (b) you are confident that your story will sell after testing it at events using print on demand.

Otherwise, I don't think it worth the extra risk and costs associated with up-front runs. The finish you get through print on demand is fine. I had no complaints about it at events after switching from initially using silk finish paper for *Ferdinand Fox's Big Sleep*. However, do compare the colour quality between Ingram Spark and CreateSpace/KDP Print for stock orders as it can vary and you may find one works better for your book.

Ready-made interior templates: picture books

At the time of writing, as with middle grade books, the only picture book template site that I can recommend taking a look at is Joel Friedlander's book design templates.

The Story Fable design comes with five different layout options for paper size 8.5 x 8.5 inches (this is compatible with CreateSpace/KDP Print and Ingram Spark, but is the only available size and quite small by UK picture book standards).

As before, instructions are supplied and there's a US-based help desk. The guides appear to be available to download, so perhaps start there if you think this could be for you – to get a feel for ease-of-use.

Book Design Template – Story Fable

The cost at the time of writing is $59 for a single licence or $119 for multiple use licence (personal use), which seems extremely reasonable if you can do this all yourself. It also includes technology that allows you to create an eBook version though I've not tested how easy this is to use.

Find out more at **bookdesigntemplates.com/story**

Planning your front and back matter content

Whichever approach you use for layout and formatting, you will need to plan for your front and back matter pages. These include some or all of the following:

- Copyright page
- Title / half title page
- Dedication
- Acknowledgements
- About the author
- Also by this author
- Review request
- Newsletter / incentive (this could be part of 'About the author')

The pre-formatted templates are likely to include most of these pages, ready for you to drop your content into, possibly with the option to tweak the design to suit your needs. And certainly Vellum (Mac only) provides the key items here, plus additional freeform pages that you can adapt for extra marketing messages, such as review requests.

One thing to note is that these pages don't form part of the page numbering for the book – they're usually left unnumbered or use Roman numerals.

The only content you **must** include is the copyright page and title page – but you'd be mad to miss out the others as these provide key marketing opportunities! I talk more about how to make the most of front or back matter marketing pages for both print and eBooks at the start of the marketing section.

8

EBOOKS

Do you need to create eBooks?

Since the statistics show that most children read in print, you might be forgiven for thinking there is little point in creating eBook versions of your story. However, nothing could be further from the truth. Here are the reasons you need an eBook version of both your picture book and your stories for older children:

- Offers more ways to make your book discoverable through free and paid-for advertising.
- Provides a cost-effective way to supply free books to beta readers, advance readers/reviewers or for promotional giveaways – also some parents use free or cheaper eBooks to check suitability before buying in print.
- Caters to the needs of children who to prefer to read eBooks, or who may read them on holiday.
- Offers the ability to embed links, making cross

promotion of other titles and mailing list sign-up easier.

- It's relatively easy to create eBooks these days, thanks to an array of free and paid-for tools.
- The cost to outsource to a freelancer is not prohibitive if you don't want to DIY.

Types of eBook at a glance

EBooks are essentially electronic files. They fall into two main categories: **reflowable** and **fixed layout**.

Reflowable

Reflowable means the layout dynamically adapts to fit the screen for whichever device the reader is using. The text will also respond to changes in font size/typeface that the user may choose. The two types of reflowable file you need to prepare are:

.mobi files – for Amazon's Kindle Store (to read on Kindle devices or other devices using the Kindle App)

ePub files – for all other stores and their associated reading devices (Apple's iBooks Store, Kobo Store, Barnes & Noble Nook Store, Google Play and all other non-Amazon online retailers worldwide)

Fixed layout

This format is suitable for books with lots of images where you want to preserve the overall layout of your content – and is generally the best choice for children's picture books, where the relationship of the images to text is vital.

For most children's authors who want to create a straightforward eBook replica of their colour print picture book, the following are the most relevant fixed-layout formats:

- **Fixed Layout KF8** – for Amazon Kindle

- **Fixed-layout ePUB 3** – for Apple, Kobo, Google Play store, Overdrive (which distributes to public libraries and schools)

The fixed layout formats below are for more specialist types of eBook with extras such as word highlighting, pop-ups, zoom and pan, and/or audio or narration.

- **Kindle Textbook Creator**, **Kindle Kids' Book Creator, Kindle Comics**– for Amazon Kindle Fire and Kindle reading apps

- **Nook Kids ePIB, Page Perfect** or **Nook Comics** – for Barnes & Noble

EBook stores – your listing choices

Note that when you come to upload your .mobi file for the Kindle Store you will be offered the option to join a programme called **KDP Select**, whereby you commit to sell your book exclusively in the Kindle store. To understand more about your listing choices, and the pros and cons of joining KDP Select see Chapter 25, *'EBook marketing – go wide or use KDP Select?'* in the marketing section.

Tools for creating flowable eBooks

As with everything in self-publishing, you have two main options for converting your book – DIY using available tools or outsource to a freelancer. At the time of writing, the three available tools I recommend taking a look at for creating **.mobi** and **epub** flowable files are:

1. Reedsy – free

Reedsy.com – the freelance market place website covered earlier, offers a free epub conversion tool from inside its writing and editing tool, which is also free. I don't use it myself (because I have a Mac and use Vellum) – however, I ran a quick test and found it very simple to use, so it's certainly worth considering as a free option or if you don't own a Mac.

You don't need to have written your book using their editor – and it's quick and easy to paste in from Word. The good news is that it will also accommodate black and white or colour images, so is suitable for reflowable illustrated chapter eBooks as well as middle grade novels. I've not had time to test how the front and back matter pages work or how flexible they are, but as it's free to try out why not give it a go?

Note that Reedsy doesn't convert files to .mobi for the Kindle Store. However – according to the KDP site – you can upload an epub that KDP will convert for you, provided you have validated the epub first using KDP's Kindle Previewer tool or the epub Validator tool found at **validator.idpf.org/**. Reedsy indicates that their epubs are compliant and so you should be able to upload to the Kindle Store. To find out more, search 'KDP Supported eBook formats' – this should take you to the relevant page on the Kindle Direct Publishing site.

You can also use Reedsy's conversion tool to create print-ready PDFs – albeit at the time of writing it's not possible to preview the PDF and adjust images to prevent odd page-flow breaks. Until that changes, I would not recommend it for illustrated chapter books. But if you have a straightforward middle grade novel this looks like a good choice – it even allows you to adjust the font size and line spacing, which is a real bonus over other free options.

To read more about Reedsy's tool go to:
blog.reedsy.com/how-to-format-a-book/

(If you also use Reedsy to hire a freelancer, remember to sign up via **reedsy.com/a/inglis** *to get a $20 discount off your first project.)*

2. Draft2Digital – free

Draft2Digital.com offers a free conversion tool that will turn your MS into both a .mobi file for the Kindle store and an ePub file for everywhere else.

I have only partially tested this tool so cannot vouch for the final quality of the output, but it is worth a look if you have a straightforward middle grade novel where you need minimal styling. The user interface is certainly clean and intuitive and it imported my Word document from *Eeek! The Runaway Alien* with its black and white illustrations without a problem. Clearly it wouldn't be suitable for a picture book, as you'll need a fixed layout ePub to retain the look and feel of the print book.

Draft2Digital will also create a print-ready PDF from your converted eBook. This is great news at first sight – however, at the time of writing, you are limited by font size, line spacing and chapter heading styles (they have style templates but none is really child-friendly) and you have no control over the positioning of images. Thus, as with Reedsy, when I ran a test with my dummy file from *Eeek! The Runaway Alien*, the print-ready PDF had large gaps before some of the illustrations, mimicking what can happen on a Kindle, phone or tablet when images get shunted to a new page depending on the reader's screen size and font size settings. Thus the free print option is only suitable for a middle grade novel with no illustrations and where you're happy with a very simple style.

Just to give some background, Draft2Digital is an 'eBook distributor' – used mostly by authors who wish to outsource their worldwide eBook distribution beyond the main platforms (Amazon Kindle Store, Kobo Store, iBooks Store, Nook Store and Google Play), where they mostly upload themselves. Owing to the limited market for children's eBooks I've not used Draft2Digital to widen my eBook reach, partly because it's too much to keep tabs on if I want to change my price, but also because I've chosen to put most of my eBooks into Amazon's exclusive KDP Select scheme which limits where I can sell my eBooks. I cover this in Chapter 25, *'EBook marketing – go wide or use KDP Select?'* in the marketing section.

The good news is that you don't need to be a customer of Draft2Digital in order to use their conversion tools, and they promise to keep them free for life. Find out more at **draft2digital.com**

3. Vellum (Mac only) – paid-for

As already mentioned in Chapter 7, **Vellum** is a wonderfully easy-to-use tool for converting Word documents to eBooks and print-ready PDFs.

Advantages of using Vellum for eBooks

The following features currently put Vellum streets ahead of its rivals for eBooks:

- Gives you the option to create customised files for each of the major eBook stores (the ones where most self-published authors upload directly) – Kindle Store, iBooks Store, Kobo Store and Nook Store. (Explained in detail just below.)

- Allows you to insert 'store specific' links to your other titles (for cross promotion) in one place, then creates a separate .mobi and ePub file for each store at the publish stage. This way your files never get rejected for including links to rival stores. At the same time you have the option to create a generic ePub for use on other stores, or on all non-Kindle stores if you don't have other books to cross promote.

- Has a near seamless, highly intuitive interface that

makes eBook formatting a truly enjoyable experience!

- As with print, offers a range of styles (chapter headings – with or without your custom images inserted, body text and paragraph styles, block quotes, section dividers, etc) and page types (title page, dedication page, about the author pages and so on) that are quick to test out and alter as you build your book.

- Easy drag and drop functionality for changing page and section order.

- Handles black and white and colour images like a dream – alerting you if the image isn't the right size/quality and offering a variety of layouts/picture style options.

- Lets you preview how your book will look on different devices as you go – Kindle, Kindle Fire, iPhone, iPad, Android phone, tablet etc.

- Makes creating box sets/anthologies seem like a walk in the park!

- Has easy to follow help notes and a personalised email response, usually within 24 hours.

To find out more, use my affiliate link at **bit.ly/VellumKaren** *(the cost to you is not affected if you buy)* – or go to **vellum.pub**

Tools for creating fixed-layout eBooks

You can create fixed-layout eBooks for the Kindle Store using **Kindle Comics**, **Kindle Kids' Book Creator** or **Kindle Textbook Creator**, all of which are free. When I tried these programs I quickly came unstuck, wasting many hours trying to work out where I had gone wrong. In my experience, these are only suitable if you are tech savvy and understand HTML – or have endless time and patience! This said, one author has contacted me to say she finds Kindle Kids' Book Creator simple to use, so it may have been improved and be worth checking out. However, watch out for your file size – and be sure to check whether you can include links, as I recall this was an issue at one point.

There's also a paid-for tool, **CircularFlo** (**CircularFlo.com**), for creating ePUB 3 files, used by many of the traditional children's publishers. It gets glowing reviews but isn't cheap – and you'll need to be competent in InDesign or an equivalent program in order to work with it.

I can't speak for the other file formats but suspect that for most children's authors reading here, outsourcing is the way to go in any case. However, if you are competent with programs such as InDesign and Photoshop and want to know more about DIY fixed-layout formatting, I would recommend reading American children's author Darcy Pattison's excellent blog post on the topic, found at *darcypattison.com/publishing/format-picture-books-kindle*. You'll also find some other great resources on her website **darcypattison.com**.

Outsourcing to eBook formatters: flowable or fixed-layout

If you don't have the time or perhaps the technical confidence to try the above tools, there are plenty of freelancers who will convert your book for you – often at the same time as creating a print-ready PDF. Below I list a couple of freelancers I have used and can recommend – otherwise search on Reedsy or use ALLi's directory.

1. eBookPartnership

A UK-based firm that offers authors (worldwide) eBook formatting across all formats, including enhanced eBooks with word highlighting and sound. They also have a distribution service similar to Draft2Digital's where they will upload and manage your book's listings on a wide range of online bookstores, library services and subscription service distribution channels if you want this.

I used eBookPartnership to create an enhanced eBook version of *Ferdinand Fox's Big Sleep* for the iBooks store and their service was second to none. I've not used them since I bought Vellum but would certainly recommend getting a quote if you don't want to 'DIY' your formatting using a free or paid-for tool – or if you just need help with a fixed-layout file. Since I last used them they also now offer print book formatting, so it may be worth comparing quotes for this too. Find out more at **eBookPartnership.com**

2. Lighthouse24.com

Run by Doug Heatherly and based in Texas, **Lighthouse24** offers a reliable formatting service for both print and eBook. He will also check and fix (or re-do) files that you've created yourself and have run into problems with. I used Doug to format *The Secret Lake* and *Eeek! The Runaway Alien* for both print and eBook before buying Vellum, and to lay out and prepare the print-ready file of *Ferdinand Fox's Big Sleep*. He offers a no-nonsense service that's reasonably priced and has been formatting pretty much since the dawn of self-publishing, so you've in very safe hands!

Contact **Lighthouse24.com** to get a quote. *(Tell Doug I sent you: note I do not receive any affiliate fee for this recommendation.)*

3. Reedsy.com

As previously mentioned, you can search for a wide range of vetted freelancers, including formatters, at Reedsy. Sign up via **reedsy.com/a/inglis** to get a $20 discount off your first project.

4. Alliance of Independent Authors' (ALLi) Self-publishing Services Directory

You can read the latest edition of the ALLi directory at **bit.ly/ALLiDirectory**

To benefit from discounts, you'll need to join ALLi and access it in the Members' Zone. *See Chapter 28 for more in the benefits of joining ALLi.*

5. Map Systems

While researching other options for fixed layout eBooks I came across Map Systems (website below), which is based in India. Their offer certainly seems comprehensive and it may be worth getting a quote for comparison if you're looking to create an enhanced eBook with extra features. I can't vouch for them personally, so if the price looks good I'd recommend getting testimonials from children's authors who have used them before going ahead. (And do drop me a line to let me know how you got on, as I will share with others.)

Find out more about Map Systems at **mapsystemsindia.com/e-publishing-services/fixed-layout-epub-conversion.html**

9

ISBNS: WHAT ARE THEY AND DO YOU NEED ONE?

ISBN stands for International Standard Book Number. It's a unique 13-digit number that's used worldwide by booksellers, wholesalers, libraries and distributors to identify specific editions of books. The number is embedded into the bar code on the back of the book (sometimes along with other elements) and is also used for things like stock control and ordering, pricing and providing sales data to industry book charting organisations such as NPD BookScan in the USA and Nielsen BookScan in the UK (also covering Ireland, Australia, New Zealand, India, Italy, Spain, Brazil, South Africa at the time of writing).

You can buy your own ISBN (recommended) or use free ones. I cover the pros and cons of this below – but first here's a quick introduction to when and if you need them.

Print books and ISBNS

If you want to market your print book to shops, libraries or via online retailers it will need an ISBN. If you only want to hand sell it directly then you don't need an ISBN.

The same print title needs a separate ISBN for each individual format, such as:

- paperback
- hardback
- special edition, such as illustrated where a non-illustrated edition already exists
- a new edition in different (paper) size

If you're just changing the cover or making minor text corrections or changes to front or back matter, you don't need a separate ISBN.

EBooks and ISBNs

If you're uploading your eBook yourself direct to a retailer it's up to you whether to assign it an ISBN – and most independent authors don't. Neither Amazon nor any of the eBook self-publishing platform retailers require one – instead they assign your eBook their own unique identifier, which allows them and you to track your sales data. Amazon, for example, assigns Kindle books a 10-digit ASIN (Amazon Standard Identification Number). Similar systems apply for the iBooks Store, Kobo and Barnes & Noble and you can look at your sales data 24/7 on all these platforms.

You can, optionally, add your own ISBN if you want your eBook sales data to be picked up by the international charting organisations. However, as this data is of no direct benefit to you, the cost of the ISBN where it applies (more on which below) is unlikely to justify this.

If you're also uploading your eBook to a distributor such as Draft2Digital to reach a wider audience, they will require an ISBN for it to enable them to report those sales back to you in their dashboards. In this case there's no need to buy an ISBN – they will provide one for free. (NB this is not transferrable if you move to another distributor, and is unrelated to any instance of the eBooks you have uploaded direct to other stores.)

Audiobooks

For the sake of completeness (though outside the scope of this book), audiobooks are another format and require a separate ISBN from those above.

Where do you get an ISBN and what's the cost?

You can either buy your own ISBNs or use free ones provided by the retailer or distributor where you upload your books.

For print books I'd recommend buying your own ISBN. Why? Because the ISBN owner is listed as the publisher of record at the point of sale and you want this to be your imprint – at the end of the day it's all part of your brand marketing. And if you use a free CreateSpace/KDP Print ISBN then booksellers will see that an Amazon company is the publisher of record. As mentioned earlier, this could cause problems with getting into bookshops.

Where you buy your ISBN depends on where your publishing business is based – below are a few quick links with a more general link covering all countries. All costs are at July 2018 and may be subject to change.

UK, Ireland or a British Overseas Territory

- Nielsen: **nielsenisbnstore.com**
- £89 for one, £159 for 10, £250 for 100

USA

- Bowker: **isbn.org**
- $125 for one, $295 for 10, $575 for 100

Australia

- **myidentifiers.com.au**
- $44 for one, $88 for 10, $480 for 100

Canada

- **bac-lac.gc.ca/eng/services/isbn-canada**
- ISBNs are free for publishers based in Canada

Other countries: visit **isbn-international.org/agencies**

A quick note about imprints (UK)

In the UK you can call your imprint anything you wish, provided you're not using a trademarked name. And, clearly, you will want to avoid using a name that's already in use by another publisher even if it's not trademarked – because you stand to confuse customers and search engines. I chose Well Said Press because I already owned Well Said Limited.

You don't need to register your imprint's name with anyone apart from your bank where you will need to set up a separate business account in order to receive payments in that name. In the UK this applies whether you're operating as a sole trader or a limited company.

Most authors starting out will do so as self-employed sole traders. If you're based in the UK you can find out more about getting set up at **gov.uk/set-up-sole-trader**. They also have an online tool that lets you check whether a name is trademarked.

If you're based outside of the UK, search online to check the rules in your country or talk to an accountant.

Uploading your book details to Nielsen UK TitleEditor (UK authors)

As mentioned above, if you own your ISBN you are the publisher of record for your book. When uploading direct to Amazon via CreateSpace/KDP Print your book will show up there and, if you use Ingram Spark, it will appear in all other online stores in the UK and worldwide as a result of Ingram's data feed.

One thing to be aware of, however, is that Ingram, as well as sending its data feed direct to book buyers and retailers worldwide, also sends it to Nielsen in the UK, whose own feed goes out to over 3,600 book retailers, wholesale buyers and libraries globally.

The reason this is important to understand is that you can, if you wish, upload your book details and cover jacket direct to Nielsen Title Editor as well as to Ingram Spark, and you may receive information about this when buying your ISBN(s) in the UK. However, if you choose to do this, your directly uploaded content will 'override' that supplied by Ingram going forward and be sent to Nielsen's customers instead. Assuming you are uploading identical content this is neither here nor there, but it's worth being aware that any later changes you make within Ingram Spark need to be replicated in Nielsen's Title Editor if you want them updated in Nielsen's wider feed.

A final point to be aware of is that Nielsen will suppress your book's long description and any review/awards information from its feed unless you pay extra for their enhanced listing service. At the time of writing this costs £79 a year for one title or £149 for up to ten titles. Given that most of your early sales will be at events or via local bookshops (covered later in the marketing section) – and most of the rest on Amazon where your description will be visible – this won't be a sensible use of a limited budget when starting out.

Find out more at **nielsentitleeditor.com/titleeditor**

10

OUTSOURCING YOUR SELF-PUBLISHING

If DIY self-publishing doesn't appeal – either because of the time commitment, or perhaps because managing file uploads and monitoring sales data isn't something you feel confident about – there are services that can carry out some or all of these tasks for you.

Sometimes referred to as 'assisted publishing' companies, typically these firms will offer a menu of services that you can choose from – each with fees attached. Their package of services might include:

- providing ISBNs
- sourcing and managing illustrators
- editing and proofing
- formatting
- sourcing and managing print runs (where you're not using print on demand)
- uploading to distributors

- royalty collection and reporting
- marketing

How to choose a reputable service

'*Choosing the Best Self-publishing Companies and Services'* published by The Alliance of Independent Authors' (ALLi) and updated each year, talks you through how to assess, compare and choose the right self-publishing pathway based on your particular circumstances – and how to spot and avoid unscrupulous services. It is free to download for ALLi members or available as an eBook or in print on Amazon and all other stores.

Complementing this, ALLi's *Self-publishing Services Directory,* also updated each year, provides a list of tried and trusted partner members that includes assisted publishing companies offering full and menu packages, alongside freelancers offering individual services for DIY self-publishers. All of these firms have been vetted and approved as meeting ALLi's Code of Standards, which requires a commitment to integrity, transparency, partnership, value and customer service.

If you join ALLi (which I strongly recommend you do) you can download the directory for free and access it from the Members' Zone, where new partner and member discount offers are added throughout the year. Otherwise you can read the latest edition on the website at **bit.ly/ALLiDirectory** (Member discounts won't be visible here.) *See Chapter 28 for more on the benefits of joining ALLi.*

Matador or Indie-Go for children's assisted publishing

One of ALLi's key UK partner members that can offer assisted publishing with children's books is **Matador**. They are well respected and offer a wide choice of services from book formatting and production through to marketing to bookshops and at trade fairs. Unlike many assisted publishing services, Matador will only take on manuscripts that pass their quality criteria. (They provide a list of recommended editorial partners and will direct you there if they feel that your book needs more work.)

Matador prefer you to use a Matador ISBN (meaning they become the publisher of record). However, they will also work with you if you wish to use your own ISBN, provided your manuscript is a new title and meets their quality criteria. Note that in order to use their bookshop sales representation service you will need to pay to print at least 300 of your books up front – they will manage this for you.

If you prefer to manage your own distribution (online and elsewhere), they also offer editorial, formatting, and more general PR and marketing services through their separate **Indie-Go** brand.

If you feel that assisted self-publishing is for you I'd say Matador (or Indie-Go) are a very safe bet and worth researching. Find out more at **troubador.co.uk/matador**

Alliance of Independent Authors' Watchdog Service

Sadly, there are many 'vanity publishers' and other rogue services out there keen to take your money. If you are unfortunate enough to fall into their trap you are likely to end up with a large hole in your bank balance and box loads of unsold books.

These companies often masquerade as publishing houses, typically offering 'publishing contracts' after a 'review' of your submitted manuscript. The catch is they get you to pay for everything – which is **never** something a genuine publishing house will ask you to do. To add insult to injury, the services provided will often be of very poor quality, making your book at worst unsaleable and at best vulnerable to scathing reviews.

Thankfully, ALLi has a Watchdog Service which investigates and reports on rogue services that "overcharge, over-promise, under-deliver, or in any way exploit authors." ALLi actively encourages authors to report suspect firms and will aim to investigate them and report back.

The outcome is a list of the best and worst self-publishing services, rated with a traffic light system and allowing you to see at a glance those that can be trusted and those where caution is advised.

You can view the ALLi Watchdog List at:
bit.ly/selfpubservices

TIPS WHEN CHOOSING AN ASSISTED PUBLISHING SERVICE

- Check whether they're listed by ALLi's Watchdog Service – are they recommended?
- Talk to other children's authors who have used the

service – not authors of adult books – you need to be sure the provider knows the children's market.

- Compare costs/royalty figures with different providers.
- Check what access you will have to your sales data and how soon you will receive royalty payments.
- Understand your 'get-out' clause: how easy would it be to get back your files should the relationship not work out?

Finally, be aware that anyone providing your ISBN becomes the publisher of record for your book. Are you happy not to be named as the publisher?

11

MONEY TALK

This section looks at how to work out your recommended retail price (RRP) and ensure you make money from your book sales on a day-to-day basis. After all, you're in business to make a profit! Don't give up on the day job yet though: this is a long-tail game and it's very hard for all but the most successful of authors to live off their income!

Note: Your overall profit will also depend on your outlay for illustrations, editing, formatting, capital items associated with your business and so on – and these costs can of course be spread over the course of a year or more for accounting purposes. Wider accounting is outside the scope of this book.

Working out pricing and profit on your print book

When pricing your book, you'll need to take into account the RRPs for books like yours, then check the costs and profit per sale for each of your different sales channels based on your ideal RRP. Depending on your book's format and length, you may find you need to adjust the price from your ideal target price.

Assuming you follow the recommended paths to market outlined earlier, your sales channels will be Amazon and Ingram Spark, who supply to the customer on your behalf, and your own direct stock sales to schools and local bookshops.

Follow these steps to arrive at your print book RRP:

1. See what price similar books are selling for in the market – the quickest way to do this is on Amazon. Look at the RRP and not the discounted price that Amazon may be selling it at. This is your target RRP, provided it makes sense financially.

2. Go to CreateSpace/KDP Print's sales royalty calculator (or use the pricing calculator inside their dashboard for your book if it's already partly set up) and input your target RRP to see what profit you would make on each Amazon sale.

3. If your royalty looks too low, flex the figures – as seen in the screenshots on the next two pages – to see the effect of different RRPs on what you'll earn.

You can also view the screenshots that follow, and examples from KDP Print's royalty calculator, in the online resources folder. See Chapter 29 for the log-in details.

Book Royalties

You earn royalties every time we print a book to fulfill a new customer order placed on Amazon.com, Amazon's European websites, or through sales channels offered with Expanded Distribution. Plus, you can set your royalty payment option to local currencies including U.S. dollars (USD), British pounds (GBP), and Euro (EUR).

Your royalty is the list price you've designated for your book, minus our share.

Calculating Your Royalty	Need more information?
List Price (set by you)	Setting your book's list price
& Our Share	How we calculate our share
= **Your Royalty**	

Royalty Calculator*

Use the royalty calculator to figure out how much you'll make every time your book is manufactured.

Print Options

Interior Type	Black and White	Number of Pages	122
Trim Size	5.25" x 8"		

List Price		Channel	Royalty
USD $ 6.99	Calculate	Amazon.com	$1.88
		Expanded Distribution	$0.48
☐ Yes, suggest GBP price based on the U.S. price		Amazon Europe	
GBP £ 5.99	Calculate	For books printed in Great Britain	£1.67
☐ Yes, suggest EUR price based on the U.S. price		Amazon Europe	
EUR € 6.99	Calculate	For books printed in continental Europe	€2.13

* Figures generated by this tool are for estimation purposes only. Your actual royalty will be calculated when you set up your book.

Example 1: RRP of £5.99 / $6.99 gives a royalty of £1.67 / $1.88

See over for the next example. KDP Print has equivalent calculators inside the dashboard.

Example 2: RRP of £6.99 / $7.99 gives a royalty of £2.27 / $2.48

You'll find the CreateSpace royalty calculator at **createspace.com/products/book/#content5**. (Click on the royalty tab near the top of the page. You need to know your trim size and page count in order to use it.) At the time of writing, the only external link that I can find to the KDP Print royalty calculator is on this page: **bit.ly/KDPCalculator**. It's an Excel sheet that downloads, so I've placed a copy in the online resources folder. (See Chapter 29 for log-in details.)

4. Next, do the same with Ingram Spark's calculator (rather awkwardly called a 'Publisher Compensation Calculator') – found at **IngramSpark.com/resources/tools**. Note that here you will be asked to input your wholesale discount price. On

balance I'd recommend 40% or 45% though you could go lower. (I talk more about this below.)

5. Use the combined information from above to work out your potential profit per sale after costs – then settle on your final RRP from there. The chances are you will go with the RRP you originally researched, but if the figures show that you'll only be making pennies from your book sales via your distributors, then you'll need to up your price.

What affects royalty amount?

What you earn will vary according to your RRP, book size and cover format, whether your interior is colour or black and white, and page count. And in the case of Ingram Spark (in my case Lighting Source) it depends on what wholesale discount you choose to offer. Typically, I make around 30-35% in royalties from my print book sales via Amazon after deduction of the production and distribution costs. For my sales through other channels via Lightning Source (Ingram Spark's sister company) I make less – around 20% – because Lightning Source supplies via retailers and wholesalers, all of whom need their cut.

Deciding on wholesale discount for non-Amazon sales

When working out what wholesale discount to offer for your non-Amazon sales, think about your wider marketing strategy. In other words, where and how do you hope or plan to sell most of your books? Here are some pointers:

- If you have no intention of trying to sell through bricks and mortar bookshops, and aren't concerned about trying to encourage online stores such as Barnes & Noble in the USA to discount your print book (which Amazon.com is then likely to price-match without reducing your royalty), then you may as well choose the lowest discount Ingram Spark allows (30% or 35%) and get higher profits per sale.

- If you'd like to make your book attractive to bookshops should a customer walk in and ask to order it, I'd go with 40% or 45%, as this discount allows everyone (Ingram Spark, the wholesaler and the bookshop) to take a cut and make a modest profit. Who knows – if the bookseller likes the look of the customer's order, they may come back for more? This discount also increases the chance of online stores such as Barnes & Noble discounting your book from time to time. I mostly use this level of discount.

- If you want to market your book aggressively to bookshops (a near impossible task for self-publishers without a national sales and PR team!) – or actively to encourage online stores such and Barnes & Noble to discount your book in the hope that Amazon.com will price match, you could go further and offer a 50% or even 55% discount via Ingram Spark – however, this will leave you with very little profit per sale on all non-Amazon online stores and will require very high volume sales to compensate.

Certainly using the aggressive discounting described above as a means to increase bricks and mortar bookshop sales is really only feasible for traditionally published books with huge marketing muscle. But using it as an online strategy to encourage Amazon price matching could make sense if most of your online print sales are through Amazon.com (and Amazon more widely), as is likely.

Working out profits from direct sales

To work out your profit from direct sales from your own ordered stock, use Ingram Spark's print and shipping calculator – found at **ingramspark.com/resources/tools**.

Otherwise, get costs from your chosen short-run printer. For a quick rule of thumb with Ingram Spark, see what the cost would be for delivery of 100 books including postage – then divide by 100 to get your unit cost. (If you know you'll be ordering fewer or more then of course adjust accordingly.)

DIRECT SALES AT SCHOOLS AND OTHER EVENTS

You will quickly see that at school events and other direct-to-customer events where there is no 'middle man', you will make a much higher profit per sale. This gives you room to offer special deals if you wish. I cover this in more detail in *'Contacting local schools'* in Chapter 17.

DIRECT SALES TO BOOKSHOPS FROM YOUR OWN STOCK

When selling to bookshops direct, you will need to agree a wholesale discount with them – this is typically 35% or 40% off the RRP to allow the bookseller to make a profit as well as you. I cover this in more detail in *'Approaching local bookshops'* in Chapter 17.

Pricing your eBook

As with print books, look online to see what price others in your genre are selling at, and price accordingly. Also, bear in mind that Amazon will always price match to other stores and (unlike with print books) adjust your royalty accordingly, so there's no advantage to making your book cheaper on a less popular store in order to encourage more sales there.

However, if you make your book free on other stores, Amazon may price match – some authors use this as part of their marketing strategy with a first in series and I talk more about this in the marketing section. Unlike other platforms, Amazon does not let you list your book as free.

Main eBook stores and royalties at a glance

These are the eBook stores where most self-published authors upload directly, unless selling exclusively on Amazon using KDP Select.

eBook Store	Self-publishing Platform	Royalty based on List Price		
		$0.99-2.99	$2.99-9.99	$10 and above
Amazon Kindle Store	Kindle Direct Publishing (KDP)	35%	70%*	35%
Apple iBooks Store	iTunes Connect	70%	70%	70%
Kobo Store	Kobo Writing Life	45%	70%	70%
Barnes & Noble	B&N Press	65%	65%	65%
*less delivery costs				

(Also available to view in the online resources folder.)

Kindle file delivery costs for illustrated children's books

For most middle grade novels or black and white illustrated chapter books, KDP's delivery fee will be minimal. However, if you have a full-colour fixed-layout picture book, the download costs can eat into your profit.

Since print sales will be your core business I shan't go into huge detail here, other than to point out a couple of 'workarounds' as follows:

- As you can see in the table opposite, there are no delivery charges if you choose the 35% royalty option in the KDP dashboard at set-up. However, there are if you choose a 70% royalty. (KDP's pricing calculator will show you the delivery charges based on the file size.) Doing the maths, you may find yourself better off choosing a 35% royalty even if your book price qualifies you for 70%.

- If you're creating your fixed-layout file yourself, it is possible to reduce the image sizes below those recommended by Amazon without compromising on quality. This is way beyond my expertise and the scope of this book, so once again I defer to American children's author Darcy Pattison's article **How to Format Picture Books for Kindle and ePub3**, where she talks about this in detail. You will find this at *darcypattison.com/publishing/format-picture-books-kindle*

Tax on your royalty income

Don't give up the day job yet – your income from children's book sales is likely to be low to start with. Nevertheless, there are a couple of things you need to do on the tax side.

Keep records

Keep a record of your royalty/book sales income for tax purposes, to declare as necessary on your tax return in your country – along with your costs and expenses.

If you're based in the UK here are a few extra pointers:

- If you already complete a self-assessment tax return, you will need to enter your figures under the self-employment pages, assuming you're operating as a sole trader for your book writing.
- If you don't normally complete a tax return – eg because you're employed and use PAYE or are not working – contact your tax office to find out whether you need to start filling in a tax return or whether you can report your income via PAYE. (The threshold at the time of writing for needing to register to complete a tax return is £1,000 of self-employed income – find out more at **gov.uk/set-up-sole-trader**)
- If you're creating a limited company or other entity (only likely worthwhile for substantial sales!) then speak to an accountant.

For other countries, check with your tax office.

Complete the US online tax interview

Be sure to complete the US tax interview form on Amazon (CreateSpace and KDP need one each if you're using them both) – and on any other US platform you upload to when you sign up. If you don't, the publishing platform will withhold 30% of your royalty income from your US sales to pay over to the US tax office, the IRS.

Most countries have a double taxation treaty with the US, which means you can be fully or partly exempt from this withholding tax, and only pay tax in your home country at your usual rate. If you're based in the UK you have full exemption from the US withholding tax, provided you've filled in the form.

I've written extensively about this on my blog at **selfpublishingadventures.com/tax**. You'll also find a video there that walks you through the tax interview on Amazon should you need it – and tells you how to check whether your country has a tax treaty with the US.

If in doubt about your tax situation, talk to a small business accountant or your tax office.

I'm not a tax adviser or an accountant – so I have kept this section brief!

12

RESOURCES AND UPDATES

We've reached the end of the *'Self-publishing'* section of this book. I do hope you've found it useful for your own journey, whether you're just starting out or are part way through. There's a lot to take in – and to remember – so I'd highly recommend keeping it to hand for reference.

One thing that's certain is that things will change in this fast-moving industry. I've flagged where things are already in transition and shall be keeping a close eye out for further changes – and will let you know about those I consider to be critical, either by email or by updating content in the resources area dedicated to readers of this book.

Don't miss out on the updates

If you're not yet on my self-publishing mailing list you can sign up to it at **selfpublishingadventures.com/news**

Resources for this book

To access a full list of resources (self-publishing and marketing) that come with this book go to: **selfpublishingadventures.com/resources** and use the password found at Chapter 29.

Now, onwards to marketing…

PART II

MARKETING

13

CHILDREN'S BOOK BUYING FACTS AND FIGURES

Before diving into marketing practicalities, I thought it would be useful to start with an overview of how and where children's books are bought in the UK. Knowledge is power after all! These statistics will become useful to refer back to later as you develop your marketing plan.

UK children's print book purchases by source 2017

UK children's print book purchases by source (volume) 2017

For reader age	Internet*	Shops/elsewhere**
0-4	27%	69%
5-10	34% (up 5% from 2015)	60%
11-17	41%	53%

*Over 50% of internet purchases are planned   **75% of in-store purchases are impulse buys

Source: Nielsen's UK 'Understanding the Children's Book Consumer' 2017 report.

I don't have a breakdown of 'Shops/elsewhere' from the table above, but Nielsen's 2015 consumer survey figures are probably still a good indicator. At that time, they showed purchase source as follows:

- 35.6% Online
- 23.5% Chain bookshops
- 5.4% Other bookshops
- 13.6% Supermarkets
- 5% Bargain bookshops
- Remaining 16.9% A mix of non-specialist shops/venues/gifts shops/department stores and mail order

School event sales are not tracked by Nielsen.

Children's books discoverability and buying habits UK 2017

- Browsing (online or in store) is top for book discovery; but 'previous reads', 'word of mouth', 'known author' and 'books for study' are all catching up.
- A book's cover continues to play an important role in driving purchase decisions.
- Price and gifting, each of which have been historic drivers of sales for books for under 11s, are losing influence while the book blurb has grown in importance.
- Series reads are a top influencer of purchases for books for the over 11s.

Source: Nielsen's UK 'Understanding the Children's Book Consumer' 2017 report.

More UK buying insights from 2015-16

- Nielsen consumer survey statistics for 2015 showed that 62% of children's book buyers were female and 38% were male – something to bear in mind for targeted marketing which we will cover later.

- Sales statistics presented by Sainsbury's *(a major UK supermarket chain)* at the Children's Bookseller Conference in September 2016 showed that highest spend took place at Christmas, followed by Halloween, with Easter, Father's Day, Mother's Day and school holidays the next busiest times. Again, useful to bear in mind for both book themes and advertising pushes.

Mumsnet children's book buying survey 2016

Mumsnet is the UK's most popular website for parents.

Overleaf are insights from a children's book buying survey they carried out with their members in 2016, which they presented at the Children's Bookseller Conference that year.

I don't have Mumsnet demographic stats for 2016. However, in a press interview with one of the co-founders in April 2017, the site's visitors were reported as being:

- 85% female (of which 78% aged 26-45)
- 15% male.

Buying behaviour

- 87% of respondents said they were the main buyer of children's books
- 65% bought children's books at least once a month

Where do they buy?

- 82% online
- 60% in a bookstore
- 50% in a supermarket

Preferred online retailers

- 84% Amazon
- 56% The Book People *(a discounted catalogue distributed to homes and workplaces)*
- 51% Waterstones *(the leading UK bricks-and-mortar bookstore chain)*

Book discovery and purchasing influencers

- Websites 39%
- Magazines 33%
- Supermarkets 30%
- Word of mouth 64%
- Browsing bookstores 59%
- Amazon recommendations 46%
- Mumsnet 38%

US children's book market

My access to figures in the US is more limited. However, statistics extrapolated from the Author Earnings Report for 2016 showed that when comparing online with in-store sales, around one third of juvenile print book purchases (traditional, self-published and Amazon's own imprint) were made online, with non-fiction showing slightly stronger online sales. Further data on this topic is limited (unless you pay for it), but what I could find suggests, not surprisingly, that the percentage of juvenile books bought online is steadily increasing.

Author Earnings Report 2017

US Sales of Juvenile Fiction Print Books 2016 by channel (Traditional, self-published and Amazon's own imprint)		
Where bought	**Volume sales**	**All (%)**
Bricks & Mortar Store	117,798,000	68%
Online Store	54, 965,000	32%

USA Sales of Juvenile Non-Fiction Print Books 2016 by channel (Traditional, self-published and Amazon's own imprint)		
Where bought	**Volume sales**	**All (%)**
Bricks & Mortar Store	35,172,000	62%
Online Store	21,264,000	38%

Source: Author Earnings Report: 'Print vs Digital, Traditional vs Non-Traditional, Bookstore vs Online: 2016 Trade Publishing by the numbers.' January 2017

Source: Author Earnings Report: 'Print vs Digital, Traditional vs Non-Traditional, Bookstore vs Online: 2016 Trade Publishing by the numbers.' January 2017

You'll find a copy of this table in the resources area at selfpublishingadventures.com/resources. See Chapter 29 for the password.

What do children's book buying stats mean for indie authors?

You will see that while most children's books are bought 'offline', there is a growing tendency to buy for ages 5-10 online in the UK. And if you're in the US, online sales of print books are also strong and increasing. This is good news for indie authors and something you'll be able to tap into in a way that wasn't possible when I first started self-publishing. I'll be talking about this later on, in the chapter on advertising.

To start with, however, most of your sales are likely to be offline and at face-to-face events, and this is what you need to prepare for at the start of your marketing. Don't see this as a chore, or be afraid – meeting your readers is one of the most rewarding things about being a children's author! And it's the start of the process that will gradually get you known through word of mouth – one of the key ways that children's books get discovered and recommended by parents, children, librarians and teachers. It's also extremely helpful for getting early reviews – and you will need these once you get to online marketing.

14

CHILDREN'S BOOK MARKETING PLAN:
OVERVIEW

In order to build your 'brand' and your confidence as an author, it's easiest and best to 'start local'. However, you need to have a couple of things in place beforehand that will support your marketing effort. Below I set out a 10-step plan to help you focus on your key tasks for marketing your books. These are roughly but not rigidly in order, as some activities you will set up in parallel.

Key elements of your marketing plan

- Include marketing links and messages (including email sign-up incentives) in your book's back matter.
- Create an online presence with a website or blog and include a mailing list sign-up.
- Add social media now or later (or not at all if it's really not for you).
- Approach local libraries, bookshops, schools, playgroups.

- Contact local press/magazines/local community websites.
- Research local events/fairs.
- Provide a free copy of your book to your beta readers and ask for an honest review.
- Research and approach children's book review sites/bloggers/individual reviewers.
- Research children's book giveaway programmes.
- Experiment with AMS (Amazon Marketing Services) advertising and research other advertising options.

We will look at each in turn in the following chapters.

15

USING YOUR BOOK'S BACK MATTER FOR MARKETING

You should have dealt with this already at the production stage, as mentioned briefly at the end of Part One. What follows should be obvious but I'm including it for completeness.

Your book's back matter pages (and in some cases front matter) offer the perfect place to grow your sales and engage readers. You can use them to:

- ask for a review
- tell readers more about you
- encourage newsletter sign-up
- promote other titles

Asking for a review

'There's no harm in asking,' as they say. Be sure to ask your readers to leave a review with the help of a grown-up. I tend to reserve a whole page for this on the first page they see at the end of the book. However, if you're squeezed for page count it could simply be a stand-out paragraph on your 'About the author page'. Do what works best for the design/format of your book.

See below for a form of words I've used in my books to ask for reviews.

Please write a review
Authors love hearing from their readers!

Please let Karen Inglis know what you thought about *The Secret Lake* by leaving a short review on Amazon or your other preferred online store. It will help other parents and children find the story.

(If you're under age 13, ask a grown-up to help you.)
Thank you!

Top tip: be sure not to give away any of the story's secrets!

About the author page

This is a chance for your readers to get to know you. A short paragraph with some fun facts is enough – look at author bios in children's books in your genre and see which strike a chord. Ideally include a headshot (which will be in black and white unless it's a picture book) – I strongly believe that putting a face to a name will increase the chances of parents or young readers becoming advocates if they enjoyed your story. I have nothing to back this up though! This is also a good page to mention your newsletter or email sign-up incentive – on which more in a moment.

Promoting other titles

If you have more than one book, include an 'Also by YOUR NAME' page to promote your other titles. The format you use will depend on how much room you have and/or how many extra pages you are happy to add. Clearly with a picture book there is less flexibility to add extra pages than with a middle grade novel or chapter book where you can even include sample material from another book.

Ways you can include cross-promotion

- A simple bullet list of each book with title, target age range* and an engaging short blurb of a line or two at most. See the example overleaf from *Ferdinand Fox and the Hedgehog*.
- Repeat as above but add in a greyscale thumbnail cover image of each title with each entry.
- Use either of the above but also add a sample chapter or two from one of the books listed as a bonus.
- In all cases include a friendly (as in 'easy to remember') link that readers can use to locate your book(s) online – be that your author website, your Amazon page or other preferred online store author page.

If, like me, you write across a range of age-groups, ideally include which age range your different titles are for. Every little helps in my view. Who knows – perhaps your reader on seeing the age ranges may suddenly remember a niece or godchild's upcoming birthday for whom one of your titles looks suitable?

I have used all of the approaches above – see screenshot below for an example from *Ferdinand Fox and the Hedgehog*.

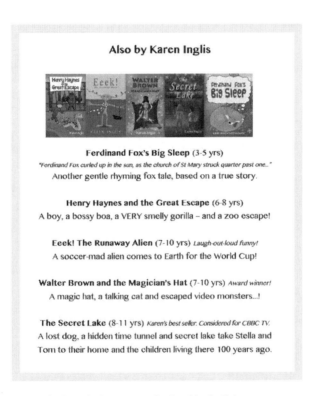

Ideally include age range for listed books if they vary.

Encouraging mailing list sign-ups

Use your 'About the author' page to encourage mailing list sign-up by offering something as a free bonus for the children to enjoy. Depending on the target age range for your book this might be free posters/colouring sheets/crossword puzzles based on the book – or a bonus short story or character diary. With *Ferdinand Fox and the Hedgehog* I include a link to free posters for download, and with *The Secret Lake* to a poster of the front cover and a crossword based on the story.

Tips to remain compliant

- Word your sign-up message so that children under age 13 must ask a grown-up to sign up for them, or must get a grown-up's permission to sign up.

- Also make it clear that they are signing up to receive your newsletter – not just the free download. The GDPR rules that came into force in the EU in May 2018 are strict about this. You don't want to be seen to be misleading your readers or tricking them into joining your list.

I talk about the practicalities of mailing list sign-ups in more detail, with examples, in Chapter 19.

Email sign-up at the start of your book

You could optionally repeat the free download offer at the start of your book – to be sure it doesn't get missed. I only do this with my eBooks at the moment, but as I write I wonder why I've not tried it in my print books!

The 'look inside' previews for print books on Amazon tend to by-pass the front matter so it wouldn't be seen here. However, it *could* help drive more purchases from children or parents browsing in your local bookshop – especially if the free offer is for something engaging that's connected to the book, such as a crossword puzzle.

At worst it won't make a difference – and if they take a photo of the download link to get the free offer without buying your book they will need to join your mailing list anyway. This gives you a further chance to try to turn them into paying customers.

EBook marketing links

Cross links to sales pages

The beauty of cross promoting with eBooks is that you can link your reader directly to your chosen landing page – be this your Amazon author page, your Amazon book sales page, a landing page on your website, or the sales/author page for your book on any other online store if your eBooks are 'wide' (meaning not just on Amazon). Be sure to make the most of this opportunity.

If you're a Mac user and have Vellum, setting up cross marketing links is especially easy if your books are wide, as you can input links to your sales pages on the different eBook stores all in one place. Vellum then creates separate files for the different stores.

Links to Amazon 'write a review page'

Some authors provide a link on their review request page that goes directly to the (lower level) page on Amazon where the customer can compose their review. I've personally not done this as it's a rather stark and uninspiring page to land on and could be confusing. Instead I link to my book's main sales page, which shows the book's thumbnail and description and lists the customer reviews at the top – I then hope/trust anyone who's chosen to go this far will work it out from there. Put yourself in the customer's shoes and do what feels right for you.

16

AUTHOR WEBSITE: YOUR CALLING CARD

It goes without saying (I hope) that you need an online presence as an author. This doesn't mean you need to set up multiple social media accounts if that's not for you – or that you need to blog regularly. What it does mean is that as a very minimum you need an online 'calling card' to which you can refer bookshops, schools and other organisations you contact as part of your marketing plan.

I still have a clear memory of how useful if was for me when I contacted the Notting Hill branch of Waterstones (the UK's main high street book chain) back in 2011 just after *The Secret Lake* came out. Being able to refer the children's book buyer to my website in my initial email was crucial as it gave her additional context for the story and a sense of my author 'brand'.

She could, of course, look the book up on her ordering system via its ISBN, but wouldn't have seen any further detail about my story beyond the title and a cover thumbnail. This is because, as mentioned in the chapter on ISBNs, Nielsen, which accepts and passes on the Ingram feed to most booksellers in the UK and beyond, blocks the book description unless you have paid for their enhanced listing service. Again, as previously mentioned, the cost of this isn't a sensible use of a limited budget when starting out.

As well as being able to read *The Secret Lake's* plot summary on my website, the Waterstones book buyer could also read about the inspiration for the story (including its local connection) and learn more about me. I'd also been able to post some early reviews there. She was already suitably impressed by the time we spoke on the phone and suggested I drop in to see her and bring a few copies. Waterstones in Notting Hill subsequently went on to stock and promote *The Secret Lake*. This in turn led to six more branches of Waterstones doing the same after I made contact – and led to many signing sessions over a three-year period and over 200 books sold.

I hope this has convinced you that you need a website to refer book buyers and others to when you first get in touch

Do you need a website for each book?

No. I don't recommend this even though it's what I did when starting out. Create a single author site with your books clearly delineated. My separate sites for *The Secret Lake*, *Eeek! The Runaway Alien* and *The Adventures of Ferdinand Fox* quickly became too time consuming to maintain in parallel, so I brought then under one roof with *kareninglisauthor.com* and now encourage any visitors that go to those legacy sites to hop over to my author site. It makes cross marketing so much simpler!

How to get your website up and running

This information is aimed at readers who don't yet have a website set up. If that's not you, skip on to the section *'Key elements to include in your website'*.

I'll be the first to admit that I'm pretty green when it comes to the 'back end' of website design and web hosting. For that reason **I'm going to limit this conversation to WordPress**, which is the platform I use. There are other options you can look at that appear to be simple to set up – such as Wix.com – but they tend to be graphic based rather than text based so potentially more suitable for use by restaurants, art galleries, shops etc. I've also been told that they can be difficult to migrate to a text-centric website such as WordPress at a later date. Beyond this I'm afraid I've not tried them and am not qualified to compare them with WordPress.

The two types of WordPress site

There are two WordPress options – WordPress.org or WordPress.com.

I'll briefly outline the differences, then go on to explain why I am currently with WordPress.com but am considering switching once I find the time.

WORDPRESS.ORG VS WORDPRESS.COM

WordPress.org

- You 'self-host' your blog or website with your chosen web hosting company to which you download the free open-source WordPress software.
- You pay your web hosting company for use of their server – then manage your content yourself (or can pay someone else to manage it for you). Monthly plans can start from a dollar or two a month per site or $5.99 a month for multiple sites.
- You have complete freedom to edit your site's code and have full access to your site's database.
- You have full freedom to install custom themes (designs) and third party plug-ins allowing for sophisticated analytics and to monetise your site with advertising and sales.
- You have full responsibility for security updates. Site back-ups may be offered depending on plan level otherwise you manage these with plugins.

WordPress.com

- Your blog or website is hosted by WordPress.com – there's no software to download. So it's pretty much 'click and go'.
- No hosting fee. Instead you choose between a Free, Personal, Premium or Business plan – the last three costing $4, $8 or $25 a month respectively per site at

the time of writing. You then manage your content yourself (or can pay someone else to manage it for you).

- The Free plan includes third party advertising on your site and I wouldn't recommend this. It also includes the subdomain name 'wordpress' in your site's URL. For example, *kareninglis.com* would show as *kareninglis.wordpress.com* in the browser bar.
- You have limited flexibility to customise your site/add code with the Personal and Premium plans but pretty much full flexibility with the Business Plan.
- Third party plug-ins and full customisation and monetisation is only allowed with the Business plan ($299 a year at the time of writing).
- WordPress.com takes care of security and back-ups.

Pros and cons of the two WordPress options

You'll find plenty of blog posts about the merits of self-hosting your website using WordPress.org free software over using WordPress.com to host your site. One key argument is that you could lose your content if WordPress.com disappeared overnight. However it's perfectly possible to export your content as a means of back-up if this concerns you. On the matter of disaster recovery, WordPress.com assures me that they back up all of their sites each day. Another historical reason for choosing WordPress.org over WordPress.com had been that you couldn't install third party plug-ins and run sophisticated analytics on a

WordPress.com site. However, this changed in 2017 when they introduced the Business Plan option, which allows for all of this and almost all of the same plug-ins as WordPress.org.

The above said, it is clearly a lot cheaper to use WordPress.org than WordPress.com and this is generally the recommended route even though there's a bit more work to do at set-up.

Joanna Penn (a UK thriller writer and self-publishing guru) has a great video tutorial on how to set up a WordPress.org site hosted on Bluehost – found at **http://bit.ly/JPWPress**

If this approach looks too daunting, you might consider paying someone to set your self-hosted WordPress site up for you then take it over from there. Once everything's in place it's easy to learn how to add new posts, edit content and add images etc.

My current website set-up and why I may switch

At the time of writing my author website, self-publishing website and the legacy book sites are all hosted by WordPress.com. I chose this route because when I started out I had no budget, only needed one website and was attracted by their 'free' plan (albeit I later moved to a paid plan due to the advertisements). I also assumed from what I'd read that using WordPress.org would be a steeper learning curve and require me to be more technically savvy, which I gather isn't necessarily true.

Given the cost differences I am considering switching to self-hosting with a WordPress.org site sometime in 2018. Certainly Joanna Penn's video gives you a good feel for how the back end of WordPress.org works and it's very similar to WordPress.com.

If you opt for WordPress.com

If you decide against self-hosting, then I'd recommend the Personal or Premium Plan with WordPress.com.

I currently use their Premium Plan for both my author site **kareninglisauthor.com** and my self-publishing blog **selfpublishingadventures.com** at $8 per month. I've found these perfectly adequate for my needs up to now, and only switched to the Premium plan from the $4 a month Personal Plan for my author site recently.

Tip: To get a feel for how WordPress works you could sign up for a free WordPress.com plan and create a dummy (private) website.

A couple of WordPress.com hacks

If you end up going with WordPress.com, here are a couple of useful workarounds should you need them.

How to include a PayPal button with the Personal Plan

Though not listed as a feature, PayPal sales using a simple button can be set up with the WordPress.com Personal Plan. Simply take a screenshot of the PayPal Button then paste it into your WordPress page as an image and link it to the relevant URL link provided in WordPress's PayPal set-up instructions. You can find those instructions by searching 'PayPal' on WordPress.com

How to mix the free plan with your own URL

I strongly recommend upgrading to the Personal Plan as a minimum if you're starting out with WordPress.com today. However, if you *really* can't justify the cost then a workaround when promoting your website address on book jackets or in social media is to set up forwarding from your custom domain address. When your readers type in your domain name it will forward them to your WordPress.com free site. I briefly did this in the very early days, which meant the browser bars read as :

- 'kareninglisauthor.wordpress.com' for my author site
- 'selfpublishingadventures.wordpress.com' for my blog

I never had any comment about this and honestly don't think readers notice that the URL has changed. I think it's the advertisements that are more likely result in customer friction.

Key elements to include in your website

Below I list what you need as a bare minimum, along with recommended additions. What you include depends how active you intend to be online. However, if you do nothing else be sure to make it easy for anyone coming to your site to (i) find and buy your books and (ii) see how to contact you.

Must-have pages

- Welcome / about me page (could be split across two pages if you want to provide an in-depth bio).
- Books page – ideally one per book, to include blurb, a bit about how you came to write it – with images – and links to sales pages.
- Contact page – for parents / teachers / book buyers. *Include a note to ask anyone under age 13 to get a grown-up's permission before contacting you.*

Recommended additional pages/items

- News / Blog page. If you're not planning to post regularly just make this clear on your welcome page.
- School visits – this is where you'll outline what you can offer. You can embellish this over time as you do more visits and your format evolves.
- Signed or (via Ingram Spark) personalised book orders – using a simple PayPal option.
- Resources – a one-stop-shop of your free downloads such as colouring sheets, posters and puzzles associated with your book / s. Include these on the relevant book's page to start with, then create this page once you have a collection.
- Newsletter sign-up link. *(See Chapter 19, 'Email marketing', for more on this and what to consider if starting a mailing list for children's books)*
- Social media links – Twitter, FB, Instagram etc, if you are active here. *(Covered later.)*

- Media Kit – to include links to a downloadable bio and high resolution headshot, book information sheets and contact details.

Legally required pages or links

- A cookie banner, to comply with EU data regulations – WordPress.com provides one as a widget.
- A privacy policy page (outside the scope of this book but with GDPR (the General Data Protection Regulations) dominating our inboxes in April/May of 2018 I think you'll know what I'm talking about!). Watch the Self-publishing Formula Podcast on this topic at **selfpublishingformula.com/episode-117** and use their downloadable Privacy Policy template as your starting point. And/or check out Nick Stephenson's podcast with legal opinion at **blog.yourfirst10kreaders.com/gdpr-for-authors**
- A link to your privacy policy in your header, footer or sidebar and on any newsletter sign-up page.

Tips for website layout

Every second counts when a visitor is on your site, and you want to do all you can to dissuade them from clicking away because they're confused or can't see what they need.

I worked on website navigation design for complex government sites for many years, and sat in on countless user testing sessions to see how easily customers could complete tasks or find what they were looking for.

While an author website is a lot simpler, I would still encourage you to follow these best-practice tips to make it quick and easy for both site visitors and search engines to discover you and your books:

- Keep your navigation design simple and ideally on one level so that customers arriving need only one click to get to any given page.

- Use unambiguous menu labels – 'About me' 'Where to buy my books' 'School visits' *'Book Title'* 'Contact' etc.

- Try to include the target age for your book/s as part of the menu label. This will help visitors find relevant books more quickly – and may persuade them to click even if the title doesn't grab them at first sight. It may also encourage them to investigate books they might otherwise have ignored if the age range triggers a reminder about, say, a niece or nephew's birthday coming up. See my author website for this in action.

- Place your newsletter sign-up link in a prominent position – and start with a call to action: 'Sign up for my newsletter' 'Join my readers' club' rather than 'Readers' club' 'Monthly newsletter sign-up'. Visitors are more likely to respond if you tell them what to do!

- Make it easy for visitors to buy your book – whether from Amazon, local bookshops or direct from you. On WordPress the side bar (which remains visible on each page) is often a good place for buy links – as well as for your newsletter sign-up link.

Overleaf is a snapshot from part of my author website as at July 2018 where you can see all of this in action. (For a clearer view visit **kareninglisauthor.com**)

This isn't the slickest of sites design-wise, but busy parents or teachers can find what they are looking for quickly, and for me that is the priority. If you can match this type of content with a more beautiful design – and there are lots of free and paid-for 'themes' (designs) to choose from within WordPress.com and WordPress.org – then you'll be way ahead of me!

(If when you read this book what you see on the next page doesn't match what you find online, you'll know that I've finally found time to make changes.)

(Visit kareninglisauthor.com for a closer view)

If my list of books becomes too unwieldy to have them all on the top level, I will move them under broader headings such as 'Books for ages 6-8' 'Books for ages 8-12' 'Picture books for 0-5' etc.

17

FIRST MARKETING: LOCAL LIBRARIES, BOOKSHOPS, SCHOOLS, EVENTS, GROUPS

My top piece of advice for marketing your children's book is to start locally and build up your brand – and your confidence – from there. By the time you're ready to do this you should have in place the following as a minimum:

- a small stock of your self-published book ordered from Ingram Spark or your other supplier
- an author website – however simple or sophisticated this may be
- availability of your book to order on Amazon via CreateSpace and/or KDP Print
- availability of your book to order on other stores via Ingram Spark's feed

You may also have social media accounts in place but these aren't essential at this stage (or at all if it really isn't for you). *See Chapter 18 for social media marketing.*

Approaching local libraries

One of the first things I recommend is to approach your local library to see if they run story time sessions for children and offer to host a free event there. This is a great way to 'test the water' with live events and, since you won't be charging, it won't feel pressurised. Hopefully the staff will know you already if you previously enquired about finding beta readers for your book. Bear in mind that they may need a couple of months' notice to set this up, so plant the idea early on when you meet them and go from there.

My first ever event was at our library in Barnes (the London 'village' where I live) and I was terrified that either no one or hordes of people would turn up! In fact it worked out perfectly. It ended up being me, my younger sister (taking photos from the back), seven children, around seven adults and a few of the library staff. The librarian, with whom I'd struck up a good relationship during the early review phase *(covered on page 225)*, even put up flags and provided tea, orange juice and biscuits! You could offer to bring cake if it's allowed…

To support the event I created A4 and A5 flyers that I put up at the library and shared with local schools. This is easy to do using the website **Canva.com** and a colour printer.

See Chapter 20, *'Free image editing tools to support your marketing'* to find out more about Canva.

Approaching local bookshops

Many local bookshops are open to supporting local authors if the quality of the book on offer is of a professional level and is a good fit. While they will be able to order your book online via the Ingram feed, most will prefer to take a small amount of stock on consignment (sale or return) to see how sales go.

It goes without saying that it's a good idea to support your local bookshop by giving them custom – hopefully you'll be doing that already. If not, it's not too late to start now so they get to know you and value your support and thus are likely to be more receptive when you approach them with your book.

If your nearest bookshop is a few miles away I'd recommend visiting in person ahead of time to get a feel for the shop – and perhaps buy a children's (or other) book and chat with the staff to find out who looks after the buying side. Take along a copy of your book and a **Title Information Sheet** designed using Canva and including a link to your website – see overleaf for what to include and a link to an example. However, don't necessarily plan to use these right away. If the shop is busy the last thing staff will want is an unplanned sales pitch form an author they've never heard of!

If the buyer isn't there, ask when the quietest time might be to pop back for a chat. At this point you could mention your book and leave your Title Information Sheet. If the buyer is there, play it by ear. If it's busy you could leave the information sheet and/or a copy of the book and offer to drop back at a later date.

TITLE INFORMATION SHEET

This is an A4 sheet, or similar size, designed to introduce and 'sell' your book to book buyers. The key components of your Title Information Sheet should be:

- Book cover image
- Other images from inside the book (optional, if room)
- ISBN and page count
- Publisher name and publication date
- RRP
- Target age range and topic/genre
- Synopsis/blurb
- Any testimonials
- Author details
- Contact details: website, email, phone

Then one or both of the following:

- Available locally on consignment – terms 40% (or whatever you decide)
- Available to order from UK [other country] wholesalers*

on the basis that wholesalers can order from Ingram Spark

*You'll find an example information sheet in the resources folder at **selfpublishingadventures.com/resources** (See Chapter 29 for the password.)*

Supporting your bookshop with local marketing

If the bookshop agrees to take your book, go out of your way to make sales a success:

- Offer to host a story time and signing session if they have a suitable space.
- Support them by putting up flyers locally to let parents/children know that signed copies of your book are available at the shop. I did this when first starting out, making use of notice boards in coffee shops and local newsagents in areas popular with young families – use Canva for design.
- Offer to provide a 'shelf talker' about your book – these are the mini book blurb/review labels encased in plastic that you see hanging off the shelf in many bookshops. I've done this with all of my books locally, and with Waterstones in the early days. Check the dimensions then create using Canva.
- Go out of your way to mention that signed copies of your book are available at XYZ bookshop in any local press releases/articles or other marketing material you produce – including the 'Where to buy my books' page on your author website.

Marketing to bookshops farther afield

Getting into bookshops farther afield is much more challenging than being accepted locally where you can drop in consignment stock and stay in touch with the booksellers. It also comes with requirements and financial risks around stock orders and returns that you need to understand and weigh up. I cover this much later on in in Chapter 23, *'Getting your book into high street bookshops'* as it really is only something to consider when you have an established track record.

Contacting local schools

Local schools offer the perfect opportunity to connect with young readers, sell your books and start to raise the profile of your 'author brand' through word of mouth. That's the good news. The less good news is that you must be prepared to put in a lot of hard work if you want to get a foot (or should that be book?!) inside their doors. They are incredibly busy places and, unless you strike lucky, it can take a lot of time to get a meaningful response about a potential visit. Also, many will have authors booked months ahead of time and – what with school trips, exams, school inspections, sports days and other festivities – organising a visit from an unknown author isn't likely to be a top priority for them.

I only say this to manage expectations – so don't give up. If you plan ahead and are professional and methodical in your approach, you will get there. I can't tell you how many hours I spent in the early days getting the correct contact names, tailoring emails and following up when I didn't hear back only to be told the teacher wasn't available or that they'd get back to me (but they didn't), or to discover the person I had been told to contact had left. It can be very disheartening, but what I've come to realise over the years is that the school and the staff who you will come into contact with are just **busy**! As a result, emails can be overlooked or forgotten about. Schools that I was convinced were actively avoiding me turned out to be delightful when I finally visited them – often a year or two on from when I'd first contacted them.

To this day there are schools close to where I live that I've not managed to get into, despite several rounds of conversations and emails. I no longer take this personally. I put it down to their being super-busy – or simply booked up with more well-known authors. But I will try them again at some stage.

Schools close to where you grew up

If it's feasible logistically, why not also contact the school you went to as a child? You are likely to find it easier to book a visit here than at many other schools. When I contacted the primary school I went to they were thrilled, and I spent a day seeing classes with my first three books. Next on my to-do list is to try to arrange visits to others in the area – this is feasible as my relatives still live there, which means I can stay overnight and so avoid a potential cost for the school.

CONTACTING SCHOOLS – CHECKLIST

- Get the name of the literacy coordinator / school librarian from the school's website or via their office.
- Tailor each email, referring to the school by name and to the pupils by gender if the context is right – for example, if your book is loved by girls and you're targeting an all-girls' school you might mention this.
- Mention any local connections – be that around the

story, and / or local bookshops that stock your book, or the fact that you were a pupil at the school.

- Include your book cover thumbnail(s) in the body of your email or at sign-off – to make the message stand out more.
- **Briefly** outline the age groups your books are suitable for and the suggested format of your visit, ie readings with Q&A and / or workshop.
- Attach a '*Name of author* – Books Overview' PDF with a full blurb of each book. Keep to one page per book and try to make the layout engaging. Again, include thumbnails, a couple of interior illustrations if relevant, age range and perhaps a notable review or testimonial. (If you only have one book then call the document '*Name of author* – *Book Title* – overview' instead.)
- Attach a separate document entitled 'Visit Format' describing how you will run your sessions and session length – or include in the books overview PDF if you have room. (I talk more about visit format below.)
- Leave any mention of fees to one side until you have spoken with your contact – unless you're able to offer a visit for free (on which more below).

*You'll find an example Books Overview sheet in the resources area at **selfpublishingadventures.com/resources** (See Chapter 29 for the password.)*

Over time you'll be able to update these PDFs, as you sell more books and get more reviews. (For example, *The Secret*

Lake was considered for adaptation by Children's BBC TV a few years ago, so I now include that in a section I call 'Interesting to know'.)

BONUS TIP – HAND DELIVERY

To increase the chances of your message reaching the right person you could hand deliver a note with a copy of your book/s and the relevant information sheets to your local school/s. One husband and wife author/illustrator team in the north of the UK emailed me a few years ago to say they had set aside a day and driven around to hand deliver to a dozen or so schools in their area and had received several bookings as a result!

If you try this, I'd recommend offering to donate the books to the school library (even if they don't want an author visit). Provided you can afford to give away a small amount of stock, the worst that can happen is that your book ends up with more young readers' eyes on it – and who knows where word of mouth might lead?

School visit format

There are a number of ways you can approach school visits and you may need to tailor what you offer according a school's needs – some will be looking for author talks and readings while others will specifically be looking for writing workshops.

Tip: only offer what you know you can deliver well. If

running a writing workshop isn't something you feel comes naturally, don't try to wing it!

TYPICAL FORMAT OF MY SCHOOL VISITS

- Introduction with slides, including where I work, my cat Misty (who is always around when I'm working) and a quick overview of my books. This works well for ages 6 and above. For the very little ones I keep this element very brief.

- Quick Q&A with the children around what they are reading, why they enjoy reading and/or a topic associated with the book I'm introducing. For the younger ones (ages 3-5) where I am introducing my picture books this is limited to asking them about foxes they have seen and I include images of foxes in my slides, as well as a video of a snoozing fox that fell asleep in a friend's garden and looks very much like Ferdinand Fox! The main aim here is to engage with and earn the trust of the children and make them feel relaxed in my presence.

- A reading from the book – punctuated with pauses to ask questions or comment on the story. This is especially important for the very little ones.

- In the case of picture books and chapter books with illustrations I include slides that show each image as I read.

- Wrap up with 10-15 minutes of questions from the children (for ages 6/7 and above). For ages 3-5 the session tends to end after 30 minutes as attention spans are considerably shorter! For ages 8 and above the questions may go on longer.

- For the older ones I also have slides showing them how I work with my illustrator.

- For the little ones I leave links to colouring sheets and 'how to draw a fox' activities.

I also offer curriculum based writing workshops and/or lesson plans. Putting these together required extensive research into the UK National Curriculum and tailoring writing exercises in line with learning goals and outcomes defined there. These took a lot of preparation, but then I never do things by halves!

If you are an illustrator or good with drama / role play there are, of course, many more options for running your sessions, including getting the children to act out elements of your story. A quick search online should throw up more ideas.

School visit fees

With so many school budget cutbacks the question of fees for author visits is a delicate one. My short reply to this is that you should request a fee as a rule, but that for your first few visits – while 'cutting your teeth' so to speak – you could offer to visit for free on the understanding that you can offer your books for sale on the day. In many ways this will also put you at ease if you're nervous about how you'll perform.

Talking money is always awkward, but it has to be done! Your offer of the free visit could be couched in terms of your awareness of limited budgets – or, perhaps, that you're able to offer free visits to schools within your immediate area. (You can slowly withdraw from this 'local free visits' strategy over time once you've established a routine and format that you and the schools are happy with.) If you are offering free visits, mention this in your initial email – don't wait until later on. It could make the difference between getting and not getting a booking with schools that are struggling with budgets.

How much should you charge?

At the time of writing the going rate for author visits in the UK (according to The Society of Authors) is anywhere between £450 and £1,000 per day, depending on how in demand an author is. However, anecdotally, I know that many authors charge less. Come what may, indie authors are not household names, so you will clearly be looking at the lower end of this recommended range – to start with at least.

Currently I charge anywhere between £300 and £450 a day. My fee varies according to the size of the school/intake per session, how far I have to travel (time is money) and the school's own budget. Most state schools will struggle with higher fees and I'm mindful of this when assessing what to charge.

MY FEE RANGE (2018)

- Full day £300 - £450
- Half day morning (three sessions) £175 - £250
- Half day afternoon (two sessions) £160 - £200
- Single session (only viable locally) £75 - £90 or £150 during World Book Day week when demand is high

All of the above exclude travel costs – though I only charge for petrol for visits more than half an hour's drive away. I would also charge for overnight stays, though until now this has only come up once when I visited a school over two days in Kent. They were willing to pay my accommodation but as it turned out a friend who lived nearby put me up instead – and I was pleased to save the school money!

BONUS TIP – SCHOOL VISIT COST SHARING

If you're invited to or are offering an author visit at a school that will require an overnight stay, ask for – or research – the names of other schools in the area that might like a visit. That way travel and accommodation costs can be shared. Just before going to press I had a request to visit a school in Hereford, which is 4 hours' drive. I asked if there was a local school that might also like a visit and they put me in touch. It was quick and easy for me to send the second school my information and I now have two whole-school visits set up on consecutive days in October 2018.

Book orders and sales

To fail to plan is to plan to fail. You'll be on a tight turnaround at most school visits – especially if you're seeing more than one year group. What I hadn't factored in with my first school visit was the time it takes for children to queue up to buy a book and have it dedicated to them. Also, because I hadn't asked the school to collect orders in advance, on the day there were lots of children wanting a copy of *The Secret Lake* but who had no money with them, despite advance notice of my visit being sent out.

In order to maximise sales and minimise tears here's how I now plan for visits:

- Once the visit is agreed in principle I mention that I will supply book order slips in advance to go out to parents
- I ask the school to send these out a couple of weeks before my visit with a return date of 3-5 days ahead of the visit date
- I then ask the school office to email me a list of names/orders to enable me to sign and dedicate the books in advance and top up stock if necessary
- At the same time, I supply posters (made with Canva) for the school to put up to remind teachers/parents/pupils about my visit and the deadline for returning order slips

In some cases the school office checks and collates the cheques/cash for me; in others they simply collect the envelopes and I deal with them after the visit. *You'll find an example book information sheet with order slip at* **selfpublishingadventures.com/resources** *(See Chapter 29 for the password.)*

How many books can you expect to sell?

A very good question! The answer is that it varies hugely
and depends on a combination of the following:

- whether the school emails your visit information and
  order slips, or sends them home in print – print
  produces much better results as many parents seem
  to miss the emails and in some cases there is no
  printer at home
- how engaged the school and class teachers are about
  reminding parents about your visit and the slip
  return deadline – a reminder in the school assembly
  a few days before really helps
- whether or not you supply an eye-catching
  reminder
- whether and where they put up your reminder
  poster!
- the demographic of the families at the school – for
  some there simply won't be the budget to buy
  your book

As you can see, much of this is out of your hands – so it
really is down to trying to establish a friendly relationship
with your contact and gently reminding them to remind
teachers/parents about your visit as the time approaches.

BONUS TIP: SPECIAL OFFERS/BOOK BUNDLING

If you have more than one book, one tip that can increase
sales is to offer bundles. For example, at some schools where
I feel budgets may be tight I offer *The Secret Lake, Eeek! The*

Runaway Alien and *Walter Brown and the Magician's Hat* in the following bundles:

- £5.99 each (RRP)
- Two different books for £11 (same family order)
- Three different books for £15 (same family order)

With my *Ferdinand Fox* books, when I had just one title available I offered it at £6 instead of the RRP of £6.99. Latterly, now I have two titles, I market them at £6.99 each or two for £12.

In June 2018 I increased the RRP for *The Secret Lake* so will revisit these bundle offers, but you get the idea.

Working with your local bookshop to approach schools

Many bookshops supply stock for author visits to schools in their areas, and/or have an active school visits programme. Once you have a proven track record, you could offer to team up with your local bookshop (with whom you by now should be on good terms) to set up visits and pass all sales through them. Both of you get to benefit and even though your income from books sales will be less – because you will need to supply your books at a discount to the bookshop – they in turn will be helping you widen your reach and build your brand locally. At this stage you should certainly be charging a fee for your visits.

Approaching playgroups and other parent groups

If you have a picture book you could also approach local playgroups or other parent gatherings to see if they'd like a free session and the chance to buy signed books for the children. If you're already in a group such as the NCT (National Childbirth Trust) – or the equivalent outside the UK – you could even offer to host an event at home. These more informal groups can provide a great opportunity to test and hone your story telling and related activities. What's more, you'll slowly start to spread news about your brand.

Local events/fairs

Look out for school fairs, charity fêtes and other local events where you could take a table and sell your books. The cost of table hire is likely to be low and even if you only sell enough books to break even, you'll be raising your author brand's profile. And if you make a loss, you've still raised your author profile and had a fun day!

In the summer of 2016 our local football sports centre was organising a family fun day based around the 50th anniversary of the World Cup. Immediately I saw this as an opportunity to promote *Eeek! The Runaway Alien* due to the World Cup connection. That day the table cost £15 to hire and I took all of my books along (as well as a blow-up green alien to attract attention!). After the cost of the table I made a profit of around £30 – admittedly not much for a full day's work from 9am- 5pm. However, I got a photo of a famous World Cup commentator, Barry Davies, holding *Eeek!* which has been priceless for PR and, a few weeks later, a request for a school visit via the mother of a young girl who bought a copy of *The Secret Lake* at the fun day. That turned into a paid whole-school event during World Book Day week eight months later, plus around 50 book sales.

Local press, magazines or community websites

Local newspapers, magazines and community websites are always on the lookout for timely and engaging stories, so don't be shy if you think you can find an angle to promote your book. You have nothing to lose aside from the time to look up the contact and draft your press release. If it comes to nothing you've at least had practice at press release writing and made contacts that might be useful in the future.

Each book and author situation is different so I can't suggest a generic approach – other than to drive home the local side of the story, and include an engaging image alongside your own headshot with a short bio.

Examples of articles I've pitched successfully to local press

THE SECRET LAKE BOOK LAUNCH

At the launch of *The Secret Lake* I sent our local paper *The Richmond and Twickenham Times* a press release announcing the book's release, how the story had been partly inspired by a magical woodland in Richmond Park (a local well-known landmark) and the fact that signed copies were stocked in local bookshops which I listed by name. Along with the press release I sent a CMYK (print quality) copy of the book's front cover and my headshot set inside a short bio. A week later they published the story almost word for word, and added a colour photo of the stunning Still Pond that I had referred to as being the source of the idea for the lake in the story, and which inspired the front cover. I got similar coverage in our local village magazine.

FERDINAND FOX'S BIG SLEEP – STORY RETOLD BY SPECIAL NEEDS PUPIL

Not long after the publication of *Ferdinand Fox's Big Sleep* I had a school visit booked in. At that visit there was an incredible young boy name Abe who has cerebral palsy and writes using eye gazing technology. (I had been told this in advance of the visit so had copied the PDF of the picture book to a memory key, enabling him to follow the images close up on his laptop during my author talk.)

By the end of the day Abe had written and illustrated his own fox story, which his teacher had collated into a mini booklet and brought to me as I was signing books. I was bowled over, as you might imagine! That evening it occurred to me that it would make a heart-warming local interest story, so I contacted the child's parents to obtain permission, which they duly gave. The local paper jumped at the idea and arranged a special photo shoot with me, Abe and a group of his class mates all holding up images from *Ferdinand Fox's Big Sleep* and Abe's book. They published the story in the paper and online later that week.

EEEK!/HENRY HAYNES/WALTER BROWN

For the launch of each of these books I prepared a short article for our local community magazine, *Prospect*, which has a wide and loyal readership and goes to many young families. On each occasion I included a witty headline, a brief plot summary (just enough to hook in readers), a thumbnail cover image and a big push on the fact that signed copies were available in the local bookshop. Most articles went in word for word.

Visit to my childhood primary school

I'm never one to miss a PR opportunity and, as soon as my visit to my childhood primary school in Hertfordshire was confirmed, I created a press release and contacted the local press there. In this case I angled the story around the fact that part of the inspiration for *The Secret Lake* had been the freedom I'd had roaming around in the local woods in Mardley Heath with my friends from a young age – only returning home in time for tea. It was this sense of freedom that I wanted to make part of my modern-day adventure as I wrote *The Secret Lake*. Again, the press release was used almost word for word.

The Secret Lake hits Amazon UK bestseller lists

With the recent success of *The Secret Lake* online I decided it was time to contact our local press again. *The Richmond and Twickenham Times* ran an article entitled: 'Local author hits Amazon bestseller lists' on an early right-hand page and the story was picked up by another newspaper in their network. Unfortunately the journalist got a few of the facts wrong as he tried to cut down the press release, but I'll forgive him!

You'll find an example press release in the online resources folder.

Will local press coverage help you sell more books?

A few, perhaps – but not bucket loads, and not instantly. But this doesn't matter. The coverage you get is just one part of a marketing mix that's aimed at raising awareness of your books and your author profile. If you remain consistent it will lead to more opportunities in due course.

By way of example, one summer term I was asked to judge a poetry competition at a local school that I'd never visited. I'm pretty sure they had come to know my name through the mix of media coverage I had had over time, perhaps a few other school visits and the resulting word of mouth. There was no payment for that visit – they had no budget at the time – but their head of English booked me for World Book Day the following year. That day I sold a lot of books and received a £350 fee.

More recently I was asked if I would be prepared to give a couple of workshops for free at a school a few miles away which is raising money for a school library – I was one of several local authors they had contacted. Again, I didn't know them so local marketing must have played its part. Parents were asked to make donations to the library fund in return for bringing their children to the after-school event. As well as donating some books to the library myself, I sold almost as many as I would at a normal school visit. The school raised around £700 from the author events, everyone went home happy and I raised my profile some more!

18

SOCIAL MEDIA MARKETING

For writers of YA and adult fiction, having a presence on social media offers a great way to connect directly with existing readers and find new ones.

With children's authors it's different as our key audience – our readers – aren't (meant to be) on these platforms. On the one hand this is very frustrating – wouldn't it be great to think that children were reading our posts? On the other hand it is what it is, so look at it positively and make the most of the fact that it *is* possible to target and connect with children's book buyers and influencers directly – something that wouldn't have been possible 10 years ago.

Your target audience on social media will be:

- parents
- children's book bloggers
- teachers/schools
- libraries/librarians

- book clubs
- booksellers/book shops
- clubs/societies/organisations with a theme in common with your book
- other children's authors – *authors can help each other out by sharing and liking each other's posts, getting to know each other and running joint promotions*
- agents – if you're looking for a traditional deal

Visibility on social media platforms – a quick note

Before looking at how to make the most of social media as a children's author I think it important to add the caveat that organic (ie not paid-for) visibility *on all social platforms* has drastically diminished in recent years as the providers seek to cover their costs through paid advertising. In practice this means that only a small percentage of your followers (especially on Facebook and Twitter) are likely to see your various posts unless you pay to 'boost' or promote them. This can be done for a fixed or daily fee that can be as little as $5 and allows you to target just your existing followers or reach a wider audience based on interest and other factors. I cover this later in Chapter 24 *'Children's book advertising – overview'*.

I shall leave further talk of the above until the advertising chapter. Just be aware when reading the next few sections that your posts will not be seen by everyone that follows your social media account – and that 'comment' is your friend! This isn't to say there's no reason to create content – far from it. Some will see it and some will share it if you make it engaging. And if your content is of an 'evergreen' nature, later down the line you can use it as part of a controlled paid marketing strategy if you so wish.

Your only other option is to do nothing at all and I wouldn't recommend this!

Key social media platforms to consider

I'd recommend one or more of those below. You don't need to do them all – better to start off with just one or two and see which you enjoy using the most. You can always add more later.

- **Facebook** – by creating a Facebook Page*
- **Twitter**
- **Instagram**
- **Pinterest**
- **YouTube** – for later down the line**

FACEBOOK*

Note that a Facebook page is classed as a 'business page' – you can't promote your content from your personal page, but do need a personal page in order to set up a Facebook Page. You may also want to create a Facebook Group to encourage discussion and visibility – more on this later.

YOUTUBE**

I'd keep this for later in your marketing strategy unless you are already adept at making videos – it's the one place young readers are known to hang out but will take time to master and you've enough to do already!

You could consider **LinkedIn** and **Google+** but I don't think these are heavily frequented by our target audience. I am on both but rarely remember to use them. *[Update: Google+ is due to close in April 2019, so ignore this channel.]*

I shan't go into detail on how to set these accounts up – there's plenty of information out there already to guide you.

I talk more about how you can use social media accounts below. However, hopefully it goes without saying that you should not flood your timelines with 'buy my book' posts. Rather tell your followers about what you've been up to, share free material or fun images relating to your book, or interesting information from other people that relates to children's books or literacy. Also, be ready to comment on and share engaging content that you find.

How to find and engage with your social media audiences

Clearly your first step is to track down people on the different social media accounts who are having conversations around children's books and fit the profiles listed earlier. Not surprisingly, search is the best place to start.

Search using keywords or #hashtags in the browser or search bar on the relevant social media platform. Obvious keywords, #hashtags or search queries might include:

- Children's books/children's book
  clubs/literacy/middle grade/picture books etc – to
  identify parents/teachers/librarians who are talking
  about these topics.

- Homeschooling – to identify homeschool parents.
- Teaching resources/primary teaching/Key Stage 1 and other education-related keywords for your country – to identify teachers of children in your book's target age range.
- Facebook Pages or Facebook Groups dedicated to an author or book in a similar genre to yours – eg Harry Potter, Diary of a Wimpy Kid or Enid Blyton – enter your search term then look at results under Groups as well as in the main timeline.
- Pinterest Boards – enter search terms as above and see what comes up. (Be ready to go down a rabbit hole!)
- On Twitter or Instagram look under #literacy #teaching #childrensbooks #reading #parenting #librarian #primaryteaching etc – to identify accounts you might follow. Also look at people already following those accounts who you may wish to follow.

Creating and finding content to share

As well as commenting on and sharing other people's content you need to have something to say yourself – be that written/visual or a combination of the two. Here are some practical tips to get you going:

- Plan and start to create engaging **written content** around your writing process/book inspiration/school visits/being a children's author and around children's books or book events more generally – in short anything you think your target audience will enjoy and find relevant. **See a full list of suggestions on pages 197-199.**

- Make a schedule to start posting your articles to your website or blog.

- Anything you post above can be shared on your Facebook Page, Twitter or Pinterest timeline – and of course those who click will be linked back to your website.

- Plan and create **visual content** to post on Instagram. This can be photos or short video clips. See my Instagram account at @kareninglis_childrensbooks for ideas – and take a look at other authors' accounts there. Anything you post to Instagram is fair game for Twitter, Pinterest and your Facebook page too. Taking pictures is so quick and easy that you'll find that much of this you can do 'on the fly' as ideas or situations present themselves. Don't overdo it though – Instagram accounts that stream endless images in a row irritate me and I suspect others too. I like to see variety in my timeline there.

- Save links to other people's relevant content to share later, on relevant platforms. However, don't just save/share an article blindly because others have – make sure it has something interesting to say and isn't just a sales pitch. Also try to stay mostly on topic (children's books and literacy if you're targeting parents, teachers etc). If you want to share the odd article of interest to self-publishing authors I'd keep those to Twitter/LinkedIn/Google+ as these platforms feel more appropriate for mixing things up a bit.

- Using the groups/people you found during your research phase, follow and engage with those that feel a good fit by liking, sharing, saving and/or commenting on their posts, hopefully to encourage them to follow you at some stage.

- Start posting your own content and links to others' content on your Twitter timeline/Facebook page/Instagram/Pinterest page.

If you do this consistently and naturally – and continue to add to your own blog or website content – you will slowly start to build followers. Depending on what social media you're using, some of your target audience may decide just to follow your timeline there. Others may decide also to follow your blog or join your mailing list. All choices are fine – and it won't happen overnight.

BONUS TIPS

For the best results bear the following tips in mind.

- Don't be tempted to buy followers or agree to follow others in return for liking each other's pages unless (last scenario only) it's someone whose content you genuinely find relevant. My experience and all the anecdotal evidence is that organic growth of followers will bring you the best rewards and the most loyal engagers. Better a small highly engaged following than a bloated unresponsive one.

- When posting on Facebook always include a photo or a short video as these increase engagement. Ditto for Twitter, though I wouldn't necessarily add a photo every time here. (Instagram, Pinterest and YouTube posts are, of course, image and/or video based by default.)

- Always include images in your blog or website posts – to help break up the text and draw the reader in.

- Break the text into manageable size paragraphs and use bullet points.

- Use keywords in sub-headings and body text to improve discoverability through search – but only do so naturally.

Examples of written content or images you might share

Here are a few ideas of what news and photos/videos you might share:

- how your writing week is going – with perhaps a shot of your office/desk
- school visits or signing events you've attended (take care to get permission from the school or ensure that

children's faces are obscured or children are only
seen from the back)

- the view from your writing room today
- illustrations from an existing or new book
- excerpts of work in progress
- news or reviews of other great children's books
- links to free downloadable content such as
  crosswords or quizzes connected with your book or
  with children's stories in general
- links to lesson plans connected with your book
- links to articles around children's literacy
- photos of letters or creative writing pieces received
  from readers or school children (ensure any
  identifying information is hidden)
- screenshots of a nice review you received
- info about children's writing competitions that
  parents may wish to share
- news about award wins by children's authors
- pictures of your cat or other pet in and around your
  writing desk or books
- book piles ready for a school signing
- your stand at a local fair/event
- an image of your book in a relevant or famous
  setting – just for fun
- as above – but with a short video; on receiving my
  proof copy, I took the new front cover of *The Secret
  Lake* for a video walk around Isabella Plantation in
  Richmond Park – the place that inspired the image
  on the cover and part of the setting for the story
- a short video of your illustrator at work if they can

provide this – or of you creating sketches if you also illustrate
- a short video of you checking your online proof or uploading your files to your self-publishing dashboard – I use *ScreenFlow* (paid) to record my desktop
- photo/video of you opening a box of your newly printed book

Make this type of content at least 80% of your feed; then occasionally post a promotional post about your own book, or share news about an offer you may have going on.

Remember: Take time to comment on and share others' posts to encourage reciprocal engagement and therefore increased visibility.

Which social media platform is best for children's authors?

The answer is it's likely to be the one that you're most active on. So think hard about which you feel most comfortable using and concentrate on that to start with at least.

The above said, taking into account the children's book buying demographics I covered in Chapter 13, **Pinterest** and **Instagram** are both very strong candidates as places to have a presence because they are frequented by women, who we know are the main buyers of children's books. Out of these two Instagram is the easiest to use and understand, although I'd say Pinterest holds the most long-term marketing potential.

I look briefly at how the key platforms work in the following sections. Feel free to skip on if you're already experienced in any given area.

Pinterest and children's book marketing

Pinterest is most definitely worth looking into as part of your social media marketing strategy for the following reasons:

- Over 80% of visitors are female – as are over half children's book buyers.
- It's essentially a search engine where people are looking to find a solution to their needs.
- Research has shown that Pinterest visitors are typically in a 'shopping' frame of mind when visiting the platform.
- Your 'pins' (the images you post with comments – and which you can link back to your website or a book sales page elsewhere) will remain searchable if you tag them properly. This means they will have an extremely long shelf life, unlike posts to Facebook, Twitter and Instagram, which are here one moment and gone the next.

How Pinterest works

It's more than a little confusing to start with – so here's a quick overview:

- You set up a profile page with a link to your author website and include keywords in your description that make you discoverable to your target audience when they use search – 'children's books' being an obvious one.

- From here you set up 'boards' grouped by theme where you 'pin' (meaning share or post) images that are relevant to the subject matter of your board. These pins can link back to the source page for the image – such as your blog post – or to another page you choose.

Some boards can be a narrow focus and directly related to you and your work, eg:

- a board for each of your books – including images, book extract snippets, reviews and relevant articles / crosswords – with links to your chosen page, be this a blog post, download landing page of resources on your site or a sales page on Amazon

- a board about your daily writing life

- a board relating to your school visits (taking care not to share images with children's faces without authorisation) – perhaps linking back to a relevant blog post

- a board of free teaching resources that relate to your books with download links

Some of your boards can also have a wider 'theme' focus – eg 'Beautiful children's book covers' – either using 'repins' from other Pinterest boards or images you've found elsewhere on the internet or in your own photo collection. You can also set up 'group boards' along the lines of above but where you allow others to post with your permission. By the same token, you can search for and ask to join relevant boards and pin images you've found there. These can include your own book images, but you'll need to respect the rules of the board and avoid spamming.

Bonus tip

Keep in mind SEO when naming boards and descriptions – include relevant keywords or hashtags to make your content more findable.

Long-tail organic marketing

The key point to remember is that it's a long-tail game. If you post little and often, and re-pin and save from boards dedicated to children's books and literacy it will help parents, teachers and others in your target audience find you and your books. Provided you remain authentic, over time this should lead to more book sales if you have a great book and are targeting the right people.

I dabbled with Pinterest in the early days but have to confess that I've ignored it until fairly recently – more fool me, given that children's book marketing has historically been so challenging!

Pinterest advertising

As with other social media platforms you can choose to promote your pins as part of a paid advertising strategy.

Pinterest advertising is outside the scope of this book but something I may come back to in a future blog post as I've only just started to experiment with it. I cover advertising at a high level in Chapter 24.

Pinterest resources

- **IndiekidlitPodcast.com – Episode 34 with Pip Reid** – search online.

- **Self-publishing Formula Podcast – Episode with Pip Reid**. *(Due out in 2018 ahead of a training module she will be running for Self-publishing Formula. Search online.)*

- **janefriedman.com/pinterest-market-childrens-books** – a great interview with Darcy Pattison, a US-based children's author.

Instagram and children's book marketing

Compared with Pinterest, Instagram is quick and easy to understand and set up – and with a smart phone you can take snaps and post them right away. Here are a few tips to get you started:

1. Remember to set up a business account so that you can include web or contact details in your bio – the instructions to do this are easy to follow.

2. Use a profile name that lets people know you're an author, such as @yournameauthor or @yournamebooks

3. When you post an image, include relevant hashtags that revolve around children's books, eg:

#ChildrensBooks
#PictureBook
#KidLit
#KidLitArt
#KidsBooks
#BoardBooks
#EarlyReaders
#chapterbooks

4. Include hashtags that are relevant to the specific theme of your book or post, eg:

#timetravel
#aliens
#magic
#childrensauthor
#amwriting
#authorslife

5. For Instagram posts include platform specific hashtags in the mix eg:

#childrensbooksofinstagram
#bookstagram
#bookstagrammer

Instagram advertising

You can boost posts and run Instagram advertising. This is really something for later in your marketing strategy after other options, and I touch on this briefly in Chapter 24, *'Children's book advertising – overview'*.

Facebook pages and children's book marketing

The visibility challenge

I rarely use my personal Facebook page but I do use my Facebook author page (my business page) to try to engage with parents, grandparents, book buyers and teachers and others who have followed me there over the years.

However, like everyone else, I'm up against the fact that most of them don't see what I put up! In my experience, how often your posts are seen organically (ie without having to pay for a boosted post) is connected with who has previously engaged with you on your page and how often. In other words, regular engagers – commenters and sharers – are more likely to see your new posts, albeit the numbers aren't guaranteed.

So, if Facebook is your preferred social media platform, post regularly from the outset and do everything you can to create eye-catching content, ideally with an image or video attached, that's designed to generate likes or comments, or to encourage readers to click a link to find out more.

Also, be prepared to boost your posts from time to time. I periodically pay to 'boost' a new or evergreen post. You can do this for as little as a few pounds/dollars and it's certainly worth a try if you're not getting much traction.

Comments and Facebook Groups as a workaround

As just mentioned, one way around the visibility challenge is through comment and this works both ways. If you leave a comment on someone else's post (say, a librarian's) then it will be seen by the person you reply to, and by others in that thread. This could lead to new followers for you. You will probably also see more posts from that person in your Facebook timeline assuming you are following them.

In addition, many authors are now setting up Facebook Groups where they can chat with fans and followers. For children's authors this is yet another tall order as our true fans are not online! However, if your children's book lends itself to (say) curriculum-related school workshops then, who knows, perhaps a Facebook Group on how best to run sessions based on your book might not go amiss? You could even offer to run a Facebook Live reading for the children there. Provided they are with a teacher in the classroom I see no reason why this couldn't work.

Facebook advertising

Beyond the occasional boosted post you also have the option to run Facebook ads, but I wouldn't recommend this unless and until you are already making good money from your books. Facebook has a way of eating your pounds and dollars and I've met few children's authors who've made it work for them. There are much more effective and cost-efficient options which I cover in Chapter 24, *'Children's book advertising – overview'*.

Twitter and children's book marketing

I'm a big fan of twitter as, like Instagram, it's quick and easy to set up and understand and offers a great way to share your content.

For anyone reading who may not have used Twitter, a 'tweet' is typically one of the following:

- A short amount of text – ideally with an image attached – with a link to your blog post or other page you want readers to visit, or (occasionally) your book's Amazon page.
- An image accompanied by your comment but no other link (for example a picture of a great book cover you've found).
- A 'retweet' (share) of someone else's tweet by hitting the retweet double arrows icon found in the footer of their tweet. In this case that person's tweet and profile show up in your followers' timeline unaltered.
- A retweet with comment (as above but you add a comment above). In this case your profile appears above the original tweeter's profile in your followers' timeline.
- A repurpose of someone else's tweet, but adapted in order to keep only you and your 'brand' in your followers' timeline. You do this by creating a new

tweet then copying the other person's tweet into it, making any edits you want to their lead-in text, then including "by @nameofperson" or similar in your text, so they know you have shared their content.

You can also respond to people's tweets by leaving quick comments – for example to agree with or congratulate them on what they've just shared.

Twitter best practices

As with the other platforms, follow the 80/20 rule – in other words don't flood your timeline with promotional tweets about your books.

Put yourself in your customers' shoes and share content – your own and from others – that you think they would find useful.

Use hashtags to help widen your reach. Users will often use search to find relevant content. See the earlier Instagram section for ideas for hashtags for children's authors.

Twitter visibility

As with other platforms, visibility has become an issue on Twitter as they curate what they show your followers and try to drive more users to boost posts through paid advertising.

To improve organic reach, post, comment and retweet regularly and consistently.

I used Canva to design the image in the tweet screenshot below. See my twitter feed at @kareninglis for a close-up and more examples of hashtags I use.

(There were two parked cars in this photo that I took, so I used text box elements within Canva to mask them!)

Twitter advertising

The general consensus at the time of writing is that Twitter is not a good place to try to sell books – and even then this would be a late runner in any marketing plan. The team at Self-publishing Formula have tested it extensively and had poor results even with adult books. If anything changes I'll keep you updated via my newsletter.

19

EMAIL MARKETING

How effective are mailing lists for children's authors?

The honest answer is that I'm not sure, and I see very mixed reports from other children's authors in the UK, the US and Australia. I suspect it depends on:

- how you got those readers in the first place
- how much effort you put into creating engaging content
- how well you segment your lists – clearly parents/grandparents and teachers will be looking for different content from you
- how often you keep in touch with your subscribers
- the theme of your books (I suspect that books dealing with, say, children's self-esteem or bullying may see more engagement from mailing lists than straight adventure stories – but I may be wrong!)

I can't say I've had any measurable success with newsletters I've sent out to those on my mailing list, but perhaps if I blogged and emailed more regularly I would find otherwise. My gut feeling is that parents (who I assume make up most of my list) are on the whole too busy bringing up the family to stop and engage with newsletter emails from children's authors – unless they have a genuine super fan in the house.

This doesn't mean it's not worth having a sign-up page though – MailChimp (on which more below) will let you collect up to 1,000 names on their free plan. You have nothing to lose by letting your list grow slowly over time via a sign-up link on your author website and inside your books. At the very least it gives you the opportunity to let people who've enjoyed your work know when you have a new title coming out, or have a title on offer. I certainly saw a sales spike for *The Secret Lake* around the time I emailed my list when the new cover came out, even though I hadn't been in touch for many months.

Keeping subscribers 'warm'

To be the most effective, however, you need to keep your subscribers 'warm' in between times with occasional updates about what you've been doing – perhaps with new links to free resources such as crosswords or colouring sheets associated with your book that you know they've not had before. I have to confess that with my other tasks of writing, briefing my illustrator, organising school visits and other promotions I've mostly found myself somehow out of time when it comes to email campaigns. But that doesn't stop you being more active!

Volume vs quality of email sign-ups

My organic subscribers from my website and back-of-book sign-up pages have been very gradual – just a few each month. The only large jump I've had was after running two *Instafreebie* giveaway promotions in collaboration with other children's authors where we each emailed our own mailing list with a combined offer. (*See Chapter 21 for how Instafreebie, now called Prolific Works, operates*). In one I gave away an eBook copy of *Eeek! The Runaway Alien* and in another I offered the first three chapters of *The Secret Lake* for free. However, engagement from those subscribers was negligible in the follow-up emails I sent, and I've heard other children's authors say the same.

My conclusion is that sign-ups in return for a free book via a mass promotion gives a poorer quality of subscriber than those you get through your own efforts – perhaps because many may never get around to opening your book as they already have Kindles stuffed full of freebies.

To try to improve the quality of subscribers you get in joint promotions I'd recommend:

- requiring double opt-in to your newsletter (meaning after they tick the box to sign up, they have to reconfirm their subscription in an email that gets sent to them – this is best practice though not mandatory)

or

- giving them the option to download your book with or without joining your mailing list – logic says that those who choose to join will be good quality leads; those who don't join may still read your book and, if they enjoy it, might yet come back for more

Whichever route you decide, let your subscribers know roughly how often you'll be in touch then plan accordingly.

A moving target

Keep in mind that your subscribers' children are growing all the time – so what might have been of interest for them 18 months is no longer of interest today. A clever way to try to manage this might be with a sign-up questionnaire asking children's ages in your first email back – but how likely parents/grandparents are to respond is another question. If you give it a go, do let me know how you got on!

Targeting grandparents

Trying to collect emails of grandparents separately through targeted lead generation advertising, or a separate email sign-up link on your website for grandparents, could prove a fruitful strategy. I think it's a safe to say that grandparents are likely to have more free time than parents – and many will have disposable income that they're dying to spend on the grandchildren. Targeting grandparents has been on my never-ending to-do list for some time and is something you may wish to consider.

Targeting teachers and librarians

It's also possible that teachers (including home-educators)

and librarians could provide you with a better 'return' on your invested time than parents. Thus you might want to consider having a separate sign-up for this group on your website – clearly marked as so. Email broadcasts you send here would have a different nuance than those for parents, and you may find better engagement. I have various curriculum-based teaching plans for my children's books that I offer as workshops at school visits and it's been on my to-do list for some time to find a way to promote these to teachers in return for an email address. It will undoubtedly take time to build up lists such as these and – as with social media marketing – you'll need to (a) create content that you can share with them regularly or semi-regularly (b) earn their trust and interest by engaging with them in the places they hang out online.

Newsletter sign-up: best practice for children's authors

As children's authors we need to take extra care not to flout the rules around data protection for minors. Yes, we are keen to communicate with our young readers but the law rightly says we cannot market to them directly, and that if minors are contacting us it must be with the express permission of a grown-up. For that reason I would recommend including a form of words along the lines of *"If you're under age 13, please ask a grown-up to sign up for you"* when composing sign-up pages (as it's always possible that children will be on your site as well as adults, and may be tempted by your free download offers).

The screenshots that follow show how I address parents and remind subscribers they must be age 13 or above. They also show how I keep to the EU's GDPR rules by making it clear that they are signing up for my newsletter – not just to get free downloads.

Sign up to my newsletter

Sign up to my readers' club occasional newsletter below. As a welcome I'll send you a *free eBook preview of The Secret Lake*, my bestselling time travel adventure for ages 8-11 to share with your children. (Also perfect to read aloud to ages 6 and above.)

I don't email often and will never share your email address. Unsubscribe at any time. Privacy policy

YES PLEASE - SIGN ME UP!

Step 1 – This clearly address the message to parents.

Sign up for my readers' club

Please enter your details below. *(Important: if you are under age 13 please ask a grown-up to sign up for you.)*

FIRST NAME

EMAIL ADDRESS

SUBSCRIBE

Step 2 – Here I clarify the minimum age for sign-up.

Choosing a mailing list service

I'd recommend starting with MailChimp as it's free for your first 1,000 subscribers.

If you get beyond 1,000 subscribers I'd recommend ConvertKit as the user interface is (in my view) simpler and more logical than MailChimp's.

Another option is MailerLite, which I've heard are good value, though I've no experience of using them.

Find out more at:

- **MailChimp.com**
- **ConvertKit.com**
- **MailerLite.com**

Mailing list sign-up pages – hosting options

The plans I'm on with WordPress.com for both my author and self-publishing sites don't allow me to host email sign-up pages on my own websites, as this requires third-party plug-ins that are only available on the more expensive Business Plan. But this isn't a problem – my sign-up links take readers to a page hosted by my provider (ConvertKit) for my author website, and to a page hosted by MailChimp for my self-publishing blog. The customer journey here is seamless and it really doesn't affect your ability to gather subscribers. In short, if using WordPress.com you don't need to upgrade your plan just in order to collect email addresses via your website.

See overleaf for an example sign-up landing page.

The link on my WordPress.com site goes to this landing page hosted by ConvertKit

How to encourage email sign-ups

In the early days of my author website I simply asked for sign-ups in return for occasional news about upcoming events, new books and special offers. I got a few but not many. Today you need to be more imaginative and offer something in return.

Here are a few ideas:

- The first chapter or two from your bestselling book in eBook or PDF format.
- A short story you've written that's not available anywhere else in eBook or PDF format.
- Links to illustrations from inside your book.

- A downloadable colour poster of one of your book covers.
- Colouring sheets using images from your picture book.
- A quiz, word search or crossword puzzle relating to one of your books.

It's best to use **BookFunnel** for delivery of eBooks and PDFs, and I cover this in Chapter 22, *'Tips and tools for sending out eBooks'*.

20

FREE IMAGE AND EDITING TOOLS TO SUPPORT YOUR MARKETING

Canva – for image marketing and flyers

Much of your content and brand marketing will rely on images – either to attract readers to your online posts, or in the form of flyers or posters to help promote a school visit, other event or book release. You will also need images of a set size to use as headers in your Facebook and Twitter profiles, or – later down the line – to run Facebook or other online ads.

Happily, most of the images you need for this come free – in the form of your own photos or artwork/illustrations from your book, to which you own the rights.

A tool that I highly recommend for adapting these to support your marketing is **Canva**. This is free to use, with an optional paid upgrade. At the time of writing I'm still using the free version – though I have benefited so much I feel I really should upgrade out of gratitude!

At **Canva.com** you can create:

- posters and flyers to promote your school visits or other live events
- correctly sized headers for Facebook, Twitter, Instagram and other social media platforms
- Facebook ads to the correct size
- Photo or other image collages to use with social media posts on Twitter, Pinterest, Instagram or Facebook

The tweet collage image on page 209 in Chapter 18, with *The Secret Lake* at the Notting Hill Bookshop, was designed with Canva.

What I particularly love about Canva is **how easy it is to use** – just like Vellum its user interface is uncluttered and intuitive and it makes image editing a truly joyful experience! It's also quick and easy to update an existing design for re-use, as I explain below.

SCHOOL VISITS REMINDER POSTER

I have a poster that I send to schools ahead of my visit, which they put up to remind parents and pupils about my visit date and the deadline for returning order forms. For each new event I simply pop back to Canva and update the visit dates and deadlines, tailor any other text as necessary then hit 'download' and email the PDF to the schools. It really takes all of five minutes. Just a few years ago this would have required back and forth emails with my illustrator – and the associated cost – as I didn't have access to Photoshop or any other layering software.

Find out more at **Canva.com**

Reminder poster designed with Canva

Free video editing services

Further down the line in your social media and content marketing, you may wish to create videos with captions or fun features such as blended scene changes and/or music and sound effects. The detail of how to do this is beyond the scope of this book, but it is possible to do for free if you're prepared to put in the time to learn.

Here's what I've used:

- My iPhone – to create quick videos to share on my blog or in social media or advertising posts – such as my walk around Isabella Plantation with the new cover of *The Secret Lake* when it came out in May 2018.
- YouTube Editor – to add captions to talking head videos I've uploaded there.
- iMovie – part of the free Mac suite – for creating, editing and exporting book trailers to YouTube and my blog, using a collage of images from inside the story then adding music and captions.

Though I've not yet tried it, I believe it is possible to edit video footage directly inside Facebook. If this is a platform you use a lot it's worth checking out.

If you visit my children's author YouTube channel at **http://bit.ly/KarenInglisYT** you'll see examples of the book trailer videos I've made. These were all done for free, following the instructions on YouTube and/or iMovie, which comes free with my Mac.

And below is a Huffington Post link to more free or low-cost video editing services. (*Disclaimer: I've only recently discovered this link and haven't tested any of the sites.*)

http://bit.ly/2K0hY1h

21

GETTING FIRST REVIEWS

Getting those first reviews is the Holy Grail for all writers and a double challenge for children's authors, as we can't engage with our readers directly to offer review copies. However, it's not impossible, it just takes time – partly because those parents and teachers and other influencers we can engage with have 101 other things on their to-do list, and partly because even once they are on board the children or pupils they will be passing your book on to also have busy lives.

Case studies: how I got early reviews for my books

1. Using contacts in the book world

In the case of both *The Secret Lake* and *Eeek! The Runaway Alien* I received 5 Stars from the ex Head Reader for Puffin UK who now runs *The Writers' Advice Centre for Children's Books* in London, which I recommend for editorial review in Chapter 4. Ten years earlier I had done a one-day course on writing for children that she had led. I thought she might not remember me when I contacted her – but she did and was more than happy to review my book. If you have contacts in the world of children's literature – or perhaps an English teacher whose review could lend gravitas to your book – why not reach out to them early on to see if they'd be prepared to read and review it?

2. Beta readers

As mentioned in Chapter 4, when looking for beta readers for *Walter Brown and the Magician's Hat* at the final draft stage, I offered a free book in return once the book came out. When I supplied those books, I enclosed a short thank you note which included the suggestion that they might like to leave a review on Amazon (or their other preferred website) with a parent's help, as it would help other parents and children find the story. I'm not sure if that led to reviews, as I didn't know the children other than by their first name – but you have nothing to lose by trying this. And if you know the parents or teachers who passed on your book you could always follow up a few weeks later with a gentle reminder.

3. Early review copies via my local library

The concept of beta readers hadn't really emerged when I wrote *The Secret Lake* – rather I used the services of a professional editor, as described in Chapter 4. But as soon as the book was out I offered early review copies via our local library.

From the outset I explained that I'd be looking for parents to help their children leave a review on *The Secret Lake* website (about which more below) and on Amazon if they enjoyed the book. This certainly worked, with several parents posting reviews on behalf of their children on Amazon and children posting with their parents' help to my website. I sent a polite reminder to one or two after a few weeks, but it was in no way 'pushy' and in no way obliged them to leave a review.

4. Reviews on The Secret Lake website

Many of the children who received early reading copies of *The Secret Lake* left reviews with their parents' help on a dedicated page I set up on the book's legacy website. I alerted parents to this page, and it's also mentioned at the back of the book. My hook was, and still is, that if children leave a review I will reply to them on there.

Although at the time of writing the review page is still promoted at the back of *The Secret Lake*, it only gets the occasional review every few months, if that. Most organic reviews (which trickle in VERY slowly compared with those you might expect when selling YA/adult fiction) appear on Amazon.

Given the above, I wouldn't necessarily advocate setting up a review page on your own website, especially with the additional rules around privacy and data compliance for under 13s. What you're really wanting as a priority is Amazon reviews. However, if you like this idea, make sure you comply with the data privacy rules. (My page is now dominated by warning messages about who can and can't post there – it's not a pretty sight and probably results in most reviewers clicking away! You can see it at **thesecretlake.com/reviews)**.

Of course, one great thing about these reviews is you can use them to promote your book by quoting them in tweets. You can also create a collage of review excerpts in Canva and post images to your preferred social media platform.

5. Contacting Amazon Reviewers

A few weeks after I published *The Secret Lake*, I read on a blog about Amazon's 'Top 500' reviewers on Amazon.com, so I did some research and found the list. Scanning down I quickly found someone who reviews children's books (and other products) but clearly also loves history and historical dramas on the BBC. This felt a perfect fit for my story which is historical fiction, so I emailed to see if she'd like to review it. I was astonished to hear back within the hour – she told me that she wasn't taking on much as she was extremely busy, but so liked the look and sound of the book she'd like to review it. I was then thrilled when she dropped me an email within a week to say that she'd read it to her six-year old daughter and given it five stars! (This was especially heartening as she had explained that she doesn't post reviews unless a book is worthy of four or five stars, but instead lets the author know she felt it didn't work). These reviews are referenced and linked to from my website, and you can of course see them on Amazon.

How to find reviewers on Amazon

Despite my early success above, I'd say the most efficient and targeted approach to find children's book reviewers on

Amazon is to look through the list of reviewers of children's books that are similar to yours then click on their profiles. Some may include their email address or a website which means they are fair game to contact – and are probably open to the offer of review copies. Or you may be able to track them down via their social media account if you have their name but no other contact details. I've done this once or twice – but more by chance when I happened to be reading a review of someone else's book and thought the reviewer seemed a good fit for one of my books.

You could also try the approach I used for *The Secret Lake* of looking through the Top 100 (or even the Top 1,000) Amazon reviewer lists, but this could be very painstaking! I think I was very lucky to find my reviewer – and at that time she was in the Top 10 so I stumbled across her very quickly. From a quick look, the Top 100 Amazon reviewers these days are largely men reviewing gadgets! If you still wanted to try this approach, search for '*Top 100 Amazon Reviewers*' in Google and you'll find the relevant pages. If you strike lucky but do not see any contact details, you could, as suggested earlier, try searching for the reviewer on social media platforms if they are showing their first and last names. If they offer a public means of contacting them there, then it's certainly worth a try.

Tip: Research the reviewer lists carefully and **only email reviewers who are a genuine fit for your book.** Don't expect an instant reply, but do follow up after a couple of weeks if you've not heard back. Finally, be aware that Amazon has changed its rules around reader reviews in exchange for a free book, so you and the reviewer will need to take care to comply. I cover this in more detail at the end of this chapter.

Stop Press: A fellow author has just alerted me to a tool called *Book Review Targeter*, which apparently can automate much of the above. However, the purchase price is $197 and there's an annual maintenance fee of $37, so only something to consider if you have lots of budget to spare. I'm guessing it only covers Amazon.com as under GDPR rules I doubt it would be allowed in Europe. Search online to see a demo and ask other children's authors for testimonials.

Children's book review websites

1. Toppsta (UK)

Toppsta is a bright and fun website dedicated to children's book reviews **written mostly by children** who have received a free copy of the book in a giveaway. At the time of writing there are two starter options.

They offer a **free giveaway for debut authors/self-published authors** for one copy, which you supply. They promote the giveaway on their site but not via social media. In return you are required to write something about your book on your site and provide a link back to its listing on Toppsta.com. Spaces are limited for the free giveaways and it's not guaranteed that your book will be included. If it's not, they pass it on to a local literacy charity.

Alternatively they have a **range of packages starting at £150 + VAT to take part in a giveaway of up to 12 books**, which you cover the cost of supplying and posting out. For their part, Toppsta lists your book on its site and promotes it via their newsletter and social media accounts.

Toppsta is carefully and cleverly managed so that children sign up via a parent or other grown-up. And while the reviews only appear on Toppsta there's no reason why, when posting out your book, you couldn't enclose a note that mentions how useful it would be if they could also post to Amazon or their preferred website as well. You have nothing to lose.

Toppsta didn't exist when my books came out but I did use it to raise the profile of *Eeek! The Runaway Alien* a couple of years ago and got some lovely new five-star reviews as a result. I can't say whether it led to more sales at that time (there was no real way for me to track this), but that doesn't necessarily matter. If at some stage you feel you can justify the budget (and that will depend on your other marketing priorities), look at Toppsta as just one of many steps in the long-term strategy of raising the profile of your book with a permanent page containing reviews. At the very least, the children or teachers who read and review your book in the giveaway now know about it – and that provides potential for word-of-mouth referral if they enjoy it. It also offers another platform to point towards for reviews from your social media feed, or to lift review excerpts from to arrange in a Canva collage for use in newsfeeds with a link back to your book's page on Toppsta. This could be a lifeline if you're struggling to get reviews elsewhere.

Find out more at **toppsta.com**

2. LoveWriting (UK)

LoveWriting.co.uk, which is in beta testing as at July 2018, is a site dedicated to helping self-published authors get reviews. It has been set up by the team behind *LoveReading.co.uk,* a well respected book recommendation site with a huge mailing list of avid readers, many of whom are keen to review books. Any reader can sign up as a reviewer at LoveWriting.co.uk

Within the same group is *LoveReading4Kids.co.uk.* This is an equally highly regarded children's book review and recommendation site, again with a huge mailing list. It also has a sister site, *LoveReading4Schools.co.uk,* used by teachers, librarians and parents for reading lists.

As I go to press LoveWriting doesn't yet offer children's book reviews on its beta site but I have been told they will be added in the next couple of weeks. Once the site is live they will be accepting submissions of new and existing self-published children's titles for review.

Based on what I've been told, here's how it will work:

- You submit your title in eBook form.
- Reviewers – who sign up for free – will browse the children's area and can request a download sample of your book.
- If they enjoy the sample they can request the full eBook for review – and this will be DRM-protected in some way (details not yet provided, but do check).
- If a title is well reviewed (4.5 stars or above) by 15 or more readers it qualifies for inclusion on the main

LoveReading4Kids.co.uk site in a section called 'Our Readers Love'.

- Inclusion on LoveReading4Kids will cost £150 + VAT for a permanent listing. I assume this would be promoted to the LoveReading4Kids mailing list, but you'll need to check this.

I think this is one to take a look at once it's live. If your book is well reviewed and you can't afford the listing price, it is still another way to spread news of your book through word of mouth, as reviewers browse and download samples from the site. And, assuming your book's landing page on LoveWriting will show all reviews, it will provide another place to point to or from which to quote reviews.

Find out more at **LoveWriting.co.uk**

3. The Children's Book Review (US)

This is a well respected and nicely organised children's books site that offers professional honest reviews, author interviews and featured showcases at different fee entry levels. You can also submit your book for a free listing, which can provide valuable extra publicity and a page to point to as part of your social media marketing.

Back in 2011 and 2014 I opted for interviews for *The Secret Lake* and *Ferdinand Fox's Big Sleep* as I had so little presence beyond my own websites online. It also gave me content about my books in a suitable setting to point to from social media posts. The cost at the time of writing is

$110, which doesn't seem unreasonable given the number of site visitors and potential eyes on your book this might bring.

If you did decide to go the interview route, again, look it as one part of your much longer-term marketing plan – it won't necessarily lead to an immediate jump in book sales and it could take a long time to earn back your investment. If budgets are tight, stick with the free listing.

For submissions options and guidelines visit: **thechildrensbookreview.com/dedicated-review-submissions/media-kit/author-showcase** and scroll down.

Visit the website at **thechildrensbookreview.com**

4. Hiddengems.com

I've not used Hiddengems but know of some children's authors who have, with mixed results. The site has a huge mailing list of book reviewers who can search by category and sign up to receive a copy of your book in return for posting an honest review on Amazon and any other sites they use. You pay a $20 non-refundable deposit to book dates to be included in their mail-outs, and $2 per reviewer (up to a maximum of 50 reviewers).

Amazon's rules strictly prohibit paid reviews and Hiddengems states that the fee is to cover the cost of connecting authors with readers and maintaining their site. There is no obligation for reviews to be left, although members who consistently sign up for books and don't review them lose membership over time.

From reading around, the reviewers are known for being brutally honest, so don't look at this as a quick way to get high-starred reviews. Again, I'm including this for completeness as it comes up in discussion quite often and could be of interest at some stage.

Find out more at **hiddengems.com**

The above list isn't exhaustive, but it gives you a place to start – or to refer back to later down the line if you're really struggling to get reviews.

Bloggers that accept review copies

There are plenty of bloggers who write about and review children's books. Some make money by then using affiliate links out to Amazon, which means they earn a small referral fee from Amazon if readers go on to buy your book.

It can be time consuming finding and identifying bloggers that are a good fit for your book, and even then you may find that they won't be able to guarantee reading/reviewing your book for many weeks or months. Go with your gut – it may be worth the wait if it genuinely feels a good fit. In the early days of *The Secret Lake* I got a handful of lovely reviews this way, which was a real confidence booster and useful for sharing on social media. Of late I've simply not had the time to seek out bloggers and have focused my time and marketing elsewhere. But if someone handed me a curated list I'd certainly not turn my nose up at it! I'd personally be wary of any blog site that asks for a fee in return for fast-tracking your review.

Below are a couple of links to lists of children's book bloggers in the UK and USA. This is one place to start – however also search on Facebook and Google. And remember to check their terms, as some won't accept self-published books.

- **fcbg.org.uk/book-blogs**
- **blog.feedspot.com/childrens_book_blogs**

Prolific Works (previously Instafreebie) giveaway

Prolific Works is a US-based site that authors can use to give away free eBooks, either with the aim of building their mailing lists and/or of getting reviews. There is a free plan (which gives you no information about who has requested or downloaded your book) and a paid plan ($20 a month at the time of writing) through which you can collect the email addresses. My limited experience with this is that you'll get lots of downloads of your books but very few reviews in return. I don't think this phenomenon is limited to children's books – but it's highly likely that children's authors have an especially hard time making this work for the following reasons:

- The person downloading isn't the reader, so we then need to rely on them to pass on the book to their child, and with their busy lives it's inevitable that many won't get around to it.

- Most children under age 12 prefer to read in print, so the format may be a barrier to many from the outset.

I saw no uptick in either sales or reviews following the few Instafreebie promotions I tried – including ones I ran jointly with other authors in my genre and which went out to multiple mailing lists. And therein lies the problem I think – free books overload! My subscribers gained that way are the least engaged of all. That said, I know this strategy is still working for some authors and you will only find out if you try.

Find out more at **prolificworks.com**

Goodreads giveaways (global)

Goodreads.com – owned by Amazon but left largely to its own devices – is a website where avid readers from around the globe discuss and swap notes about books, create reading lists and leave book ratings and reviews. Think global reading club. Any reader who signs up can leave a book review on Goodreads so it's worth mentioning it as an option when sending out review copies.

In return for a fee the platform allows you to offer your book in a giveaway to help raise its profile and (hopefully) garner reviews. Site visitors coming to the Goodreads' giveaway page can search by genre and by country in which the giveaway is available (you decide this) then sign up for their name to go into the draw. You choose how long to list the giveaway for – the longer the listing time, the greater the number of people who may add your book to their 'TBR' (to be read) pile in the meantime and so help raise your book's profile visually on a site that's visited by thousands of readers every day.

Goodreads giveaways were free to take part in until late 2017 and proved very useful for me in the early days. I gave away 3-5 print books each time and, in each case, sent a hand signed copy with a card and short note asking if the winner would mind leaving a review online – ideally on both Goodreads and Amazon. This worked well for *The Secret Lake, Ferdinand Fox's Big Sleep* and *Eeek! The Runaway Alien*. However, with *Walter Brown and the Magician's Hat* I had less luck – and by that time was starting to hear stories of people failing to get reviews. There is a perception – which may or may not be correct – that there are now a lot of people who sign up for Goodreads giveaways just to get hold of a new book that they can re-sell online. At the time of writing it costs $119 to run a giveaway. Personally I'd use this as a last resort option and am really only including it here for completeness.

To find out more visit **Goodreads.com**

Amazon giveaway

I've not tried these, nor have I heard many authors sing their praises – and given the barriers we already have marketing children's books I would put this a long way down the 'to investigate' list. However, much later down the line when you have a good number of reviews against your book/s they could be useful for brand awareness building, especially if you're writing a series. Why? Because, according to the article below, anyone who signs up for your free book in an Amazon giveaway automatically becomes your follower, and so is notified by email when you bring out a new book. Food for later thought I'd say! Find out more at **http://bit.ly/2l6Ckes** (*Caveat: this article is from 2016, so some of the facts may be out of date but it's the best I could find.*)

You can read Amazon's own information about giveaways at **amazon.com/b?node=11715260011** or search online.

Advance reader reviews – latest Amazon rules

Note that the changes I mention below may have evolved by the time you come to read this, so always check online. At the time of writing there is still some confusion around whether the rules apply to book reviews. What is certain is that some authors, both traditional and self-published, have seen reviews removed or disallowed recently.

In the traditional world publishers have for many years obtained early reviews for new titles by providing ARCs (advance reader copies) to selected readers who are keen reviewers and/or to other authors in a similar genre. ARCs are provided ahead of the official publication date so that by the time the book is released there are already reviews in the press or online – or these quickly appear online soon after launch.

Self-published authors have been using a similar method to get early reviews on Amazon and elsewhere in recent years – and rightly so. This is how the publishing industry has always worked and, provided the reviewer makes clear they received a free copy in exchange for an honest review, the practice is within Amazon's rules.

Alongside this approach, and since Amazon introduced the **'verified purchase'** badge against reviews a few years ago, some authors have offered a time-limited reduced price of the eBook version of a new title to enable advance readers to leave 'verified purchase' reviews soon after launch after buying the book for 99c/99p.

However, in the early summer of 2018 Amazon updated its guidelines to introduce the following restrictions around reviews.

- It is limiting how many 'non-verified purchase' reviews a single reviewer can leave to no more than five in a week.
- It now requires non-verified purchase reviewers to have spent a minimum of $50/£40 on Amazon in the last 12 months.
- Its guidelines also seem to suggest that where a large number of verified reviews appear at a book's launch, some of these may be removed in the interests of transparency if it suspects that an artificially low and short-lived introductory price on an eBook was used solely to get those verified reviews. (This is my interpretation at least.)

Confusingly, the wording as at July 2018 suggests that these rules might not apply at all to digital or print books – just other products.

And, indeed Amazon's community guidelines at the time of writing say: *"Book authors and publishers may continue to provide free or discounted copies of their books to readers, as long as the author or publisher does not require a review in exchange or attempt to influence the review."*

However, author reports of advance reviews being taken down, or their advance reviewers not being able to post due to not having spent money on Amazon in the past 12 months, or due to having reached their review limit would suggest otherwise.

TIPS TO MINIMISE LOSS OF REVIEWS

- Don't ask family members or close friends to leave reviews – Amazon somehow works this out.
- If sharing links to your book, keep them clean – ie strip them back to the book's 10-digit Amazon identifier number that comes directly after the book title. (The information that comes after this may include data that links the original search back to you. Amazon may then make the assumption that you are sharing the link with a family member or close friend even if that's not the case.)
- Don't try to influence reviewers or **require** them to leave a review in return for a free or discounted copy of your book.
- It may be wise to ask for reviews to be posted

elsewhere as well as on Amazon – to avoid the risk
of losing them altogether – forewarned is forearmed!
Goodreads is the obvious choice here.

- If you have a large reader team or mailing list, you
  might also want to look at staggering review
  requests or launch emails to avoid Amazon flagging
  unusual behaviour on your account and unfairly
  removing reviews.

The rules may have changed or been further clarified by the
time you read this. Either way, if you plan a strategic launch
involving a lot of advance reviewers, I'd strongly
recommend searching in author forums to check the latest
rules and facts.

22

TIPS AND TOOLS FOR SENDING EBOOK REVIEW COPIES

Send a Word document to Kindle

If you want to supply an eBook copy of your book for review before it's been formatted for Kindle, a quick and easy way to do this is to email the reviewer a Word document to their Kindle address. It will then magically appear ready to read on their device.

For this to work they need to 'allow' their Kindle to accept an email from you. This is easy to set up, but they probably won't know how. Here are some handy instructions that you can send them:

READER INSTRUCTIONS

1. Go to Amazon and log into your account.
2. Under 'Your Account' (top right on a desk top) click on 'Manage your content and devices'.

3. Choose the tab / link 'Preferences' or 'Settings' (it's one of four links towards the top of the page).

4. Scroll down and click on 'Personal document settings' (it's the 7th or so heading about half way down).

5. Under 'Send to Kindle-Email Settings', you will see your Kindle's email address (if you have more than one Kindle there will be more than one email address).

6. Copy the email address for the Kindle you want to read the manuscript on and send it to me once you've completed Step 7.

7. Under 'Approved document email list' click on 'Add new approved email address' and enter my email address which is [author insert your email address here]. My email address will now appear in your approved list.

8. Now email me your Kindle's address that you copied at Step 6.

AUTHOR ACTION

Email your Word document to the reader's Kindle address in the normal way as an attachment. You don't need to include a subject line, but you can if you wish. The book will appear on their Kindle's home page when they next sync it – with a placeholder cover based on the file name.

Using BookFunnel to deliver eBooks

BookFunnel is a fantastic service that enables authors to send readers free eBooks quickly and seamlessly. If you're planning to share eBooks as part of a launch strategy or a more general giveaway, don't let this pass you by! You can also use BookFunnel to sell your eBook.

Their First-Time Author Plan at $20 per year should more than meet your needs to begin with. Once you're ready to expand your marketing the Mid-List Plan ($10 a month or $100 a year at the time of writing) is still excellent value.

Here's how it works:

- You upload an ePub, .mobi and (optional) PDF version of your book to BookFunnel – see Chapter 8 for how to create the eBook files.
- Once the files are uploaded you follow their simple instructions to create a book landing page, with a brief description and cover image.
- Once the landing page is ready you can generate as many separate links to it as you wish for segmented marketing purposes.
- You then market these links to readers (or email the link to readers who have agreed to read and review your book).
- When a reader clicks on the link you sent them, BookFunnel handholds them through choosing the right file format for their eReader (*ePub* for phone or tablet, *.mobi* for Kindle or *PDF* for desktop reading or printing) then guides them through how to get the file onto their device.

Using BookFunnel for joint promotions

If you choose the Mid-List Plan you can also run giveaways and/or joint promotions with other authors and collect email addresses.

Using BookFunnel Print Codes to sell or give away eBooks at events

Stop Press: BookFunnel introduced Print Codes in July 2018. I am including them here for completeness. Their use extends beyond delivery of free review copies.

In July 2018 BookFunnel introduced unique, non-sharable Print Codes to use on flyers, bookmarks and other marketing material as a way to give away or sell your eBook in person at events. You need to be on BookFunnel's Mid-List Plan to use this service. (I'm guessing that you could, alternatively, print the codes onto paper as tear-off slips, perhaps using Canva to brand the slips.)

At the point of download you can give the reader the chance to sign up to your email list.

One thought is that providing a unique code on each flyer or bookmark is likely to be costly. If so, as a workaround you could print or hand-write the codes onto coloured labels at home and add these to your hand-outs.

Children's authors might use these BookFunnel Print Codes at local fairs or bookshop/library readings, or in hand-outs after a school visit, for example. However, bear in mind that you'll need to adapt any email sign-up message to ensure that it's the parent and not the child that signs up to your list – as described in Chapter 19 on email marketing.

Of course, if you're on BookFunnel's First-Time Author Plan you can choose to use a single shareable code in the same way to give away eBooks without collecting email addresses. In this case there is no issue with extra print costs for having the code within the flyer or bookmark, because the design won't vary. Similarly, you could use this single shareable code method with the Mid-List Author Plan and give readers the *option* to sign up to your list.

Coming back to BookFunnel's core offer, I love good web design and they come up trumps in removing what was once a huge headache for writers trying to share eBooks with readers, only to find that they didn't understand how to get the files they'd received onto their reading device!

To find out more, visit **BookFunnel.com**

23

GETTING YOUR BOOK INTO HIGH STREET BOOKSHOPS

I've left this section until late on deliberately, as I don't believe it viable for most self-published authors to achieve many sales across high street bookshops beyond their local or near-local stores. Moreover, trying to get your books widely stocked comes with financial risks.

Barriers and risks around getting into high street bookshops

I shall start with the challenges. However, it's not all bad news! The next section looks at a workaround in the UK that may help if you have a strong track record and know you will be able sell any returned stock if things don't work out.

BARRIERS

- Unless you have an established sales track record or the backing of a publicist then booksellers are unlikely to order your book, even if you tell them about it. Shelf space is limited and they want to order what they know will sell.

- They also know that readers are unlikely to come looking for your book if you aren't known already, or part of an established publishing house that may be helping raise your profile in the background.
- Most traditional publishers have a national sales team that sells into bookshops at face-to-face visits. With the larger chain stores these sorts of deals are done at a centralised level. Trying to compete with this will be extremely difficult.
- At the time of writing, bookshops' ordering systems typically show print-on-demand titles as having a long delivery time (often a few weeks) even though they are usually printed within 48 hours of the order. This is all down to delays in the supply chain between the printer/distributor, the wholesaler and (in some cases) bookshops' own centralised distribution hubs. Thus, even if a bookshop took an interest, the ordering timeline would throw up an instant barrier – as well as the risk of losing the sale to Amazon while waiting for the order to come in.

Risks

- Most bookshops won't stock a book they can't return – which means you'd need to accept returns and the associated costs. (Of course, if a customer places an order that's a different matter – but see last bullet above.)
- If you were serious about trying to get into multiple

stores you'd need to print a lot of stock up front. How would you cope financially if it all got returned?

- You'd either need to pay a substantial amount for sales and publicity support, or spend considerable time and money yourself mailing and/or emailing bookshops to tell them about your book – and ditto for national media to raise your book's profile.

- Historically, publishers have paid the major high street book chains to have their books placed on bookshop tables and/or face out displays. While some booksellers may have moved away from this strategy to one more closely based on what customers want/are buying, they are still more likely to offer these spaces to traditionally published books that are supported by strong marketing budgets as they know that people will come looking for these titles. So, even with all the efforts above, there's a strong risk that very few people will find and buy your book.

In short, trying to get into non-local bookshops only makes sense if you have a strong marketing campaign and/or very strong online sales that have led to word-of-mouth publicity meaning that both readers and booksellers have your title on their radar. Only then might it be worth printing stock up front and taking the risk of allowing returns.

Clays UK printers helping self-publishers and bookshops

The above all said, there is one solution in the UK that gets around part of the problem – using Clays printers to make it quick and easy for bookshops to order your book. This option could make sense if you have evidence of demand and have a back-up plan to sell returned stock if necessary. For example, if you have a book that sells well in schools, this could be your back-up. (Note that Clays doesn't offer full colour printing at the time of writing, so this will not work for picture books.)

How the Clays arrangement works

Clays here in the UK (**clays.co.uk**) – are printers for many traditional publishers, including Nosy Crow and Hodder to name just a couple.

As well as offering digital short runs alongside their offset longer-run printing service for larger clients, Clays also has a great set-up for small and self-publishers to make ordering by high street bookshops easier. In short, they will hold up to 70 of your short-run books in their warehouse and send up to 30 to Gardners wholesalers using a special distribution arrangement they have with them.

If you sign up for this service, it means that UK bookshops who use Gardners (by far the majority) will see your book as being 'in stock' on their till's data feed.

As a result, provided they know about your book (and this is where my earlier caveat about marketing campaigns comes in), this gives it a far higher chance of being ordered than if they see it as being on several weeks' delivery, which a print-on-demand title typically shows.

Fees and wholesale discount

Note that this is a specific distribution arrangement that Clays has with Gardners. At the time of writing the key things to know are:

- you need to offer a 50% discount off the RRP of your book to Gardners
- Clays takes 6% of your RRP for each sale
- you receive 44% royalties less the print cost for each book sold

This is not a bad deal by any means. However (to emphasise the point yet again) it really only makes sense if you raise awareness of your book through a concerted sales and/or marketing campaign – and/or if your book is already selling well on Amazon to the extent that word of mouth means customers may start asking for it. If this isn't the case, it's unlikely that either booksellers – or browsing customers in the shops you do manage to get into – will end up noticing and buying your book.

Case study: The Secret Lake with Clays

At the time of writing I'm running an experiment making *The Secret Lake* available on a returns-allowed basis through the Clays/Gardners arrangement. I have decided to try this for three reasons:

1. *The Secret Lake* has been in the Amazon children's book bestseller lists for a few weeks now – so I'm hoping word of mouth might raise its profile beyond

Amazon buyers. (In fact it reached 75 in the whole of the Amazon UK store at one point in July 2018.)

2. I was due to top up my own stock anyway. Instead of using Lightning Source, this time I used Clays for an order of 200. They have kept 100, of which 30 have gone to Gardners. I have the remaining 100 here, which I will use to supply my local bookshop, as usual, and at future school visits.

3. If things don't go to plan and books are returned, I know I can sell them at school events – and the cost of posting returns is not charged to me.

My plan is to keep promoting *The Secret Lake* not just through advertising but also on a gradual drip feed basis to more and more bookshops outside my immediate area. Follow my blog at **selfpublishingadventures.com** or sign up to my newsletter there for reports of how it's going.

The print cost for 200 with Clays came in lower per unit than with Lightning Source, as expected. However, my profit per sale will be less than on Amazon by around £1 per book. This is understandable as there's now a wholesaler in the supply chain, but if it leads to more book sales everyone's still better off.

Stop Press: Just before going to print with this book over 40 orders had been placed by bookshops via Gardners over a space of three weeks. I'm guessing these are requests from customers who've discovered *The Secret Lake* through word of mouth as a result of the Amazon sales, as I've not yet had time to promote it to booksellers owing to my deadline with this book!

Further essential reading on getting into bookshops

For an in-depth look at getting into bookshops, see *'How to Get Your Self-Published Book into Bookstores'* by Debbie Young, published by the Alliance of Independent Authors (ALLi).

The above is available in print or as an eBook online – or you can download it for free along with many other useful guides if you're a member of ALLi. *See Chapter 28 for the benefits of joining ALLi.*

Also, see the UK's Booksellers Association 2017 handy guide to getting into bookshops here: **bit.ly/bookshopsguide**

24

CHILDREN'S BOOK ADVERTISING: OVERVIEW

When I first planned this book a couple of years ago I hadn't intended to include a section on advertising. At that time the only obvious platform to try was Facebook and this wasn't working for me or for most children's authors I knew. However, things have changed significantly since then, so I shall include an overview section here.

What I set out below is not a nuts and bolts 'how to' guide, though I may produce one for children's authors at some stage. If you want more detail, there's lots of free information out there, as well as the paid-for 'Ads for Authors' course from **selfpublisingforumula.com**.

For all of these forms of advertising, you need to set up a business account with the relevant platform.

1. Facebook advertising

I first experimented with simple Facebook ads way back in 2013, spending $5 a day over a week or so aiming mainly for page likes for *The Secret Lake,* as everything I had read told me that Facebook users didn't like being taken off the platform. The page got lots of likes, but I really wasn't sure what to do with them and was still busy in my day job in any event! I also ran a few ads to the book's Amazon page. With no obvious impact on sales, I shelved the idea.

I tried again in 2016/2017 by which time the range of ads types had become more sophisticated, offering not just single images but also carousal ads, video ads, lead generation ads, awareness ads, website traffic and conversion ads and so on.

Audience targeting had also become more sophisticated, giving you the option to narrow down not just by location and demographic but also by interest and buying behaviour. However, while this form of advertising has worked extremely well for many authors of adult and YA books it continues to be a challenge for me (and for most children's authors I know who have tried it). I think this comes back to the fact that those we are targeting are not the book readers and so impulse buys are much harder to come by. The parent 'busyness factor' may also play a role, combined with the fact they are not on Facebook to buy books.

Buyer beware

Facebook has a wonderful knack of eating your money and costs per click have risen significantly in the last couple of years, so this is a space that I still treat with caution. Almost the only instance I've heard of where it has worked for children's books is for the 'Lost My Name' personalised books published by Wonderbly, which have apparently sold millions off the back of Facebook ads. However, their marketing budget is huge (really huge). Interestingly, at a presentation I went to at the London Book Fair 2018, Wonderbly remarked on the rising cost of gaining customers via Facebook, implying it may not be sustainable. That apart, the only other success I'm aware of is with a small independent children's publisher in the USA which drives high numbers of likes and engagement with their ads (and this presumably has knock-on for sales).

Keep it simple with boosted posts

I don't profess to be an expert on this, but my personal view when it comes to children's authors is that, for now, Facebook advertising is most useful for occasionally boosting posts from your author Facebook page. As described earlier, this helps to keep you on your followers' radars and will hopefully drive organic sales and new page likes. In this mix you could include the odd promotional piece about one of your books, widening those boosts to friends of your followers or audiences with interests that make them good candidates for your books. New audiences that engage by liking your booted post can then be invited to like your page.

It's reasonably easy to follow the instructions on Facebook to do this. Just be sure to put a cap on how much you want to spend per day and set a start and end date!

Tip: the value of lookalike audiences

It is worth taking every opportunity to get genuinely interested people to like your page, because Facebook can create 'Lookalike' audiences of your page that you may want to call on later for more active 'brand awareness' Facebook advertising.

My instinct tells me that brand awareness advertising might work well as part of a wider advertising campaign much further down the line, when your book has lots of reviews, is selling well and you have budget to spare. I should stress that this is just my hunch. I've not run the numbers but suspect costs to run this type of ad would be a lot lower than for ads designed to generate leads or sales.

2. Instagram advertising

Instagram ads can be run as part of a Facebook ad campaign – you set up the ad in your Facebook ads manager and opt to include Instagram as one of the placements. Or you can promote Instagram posts on a pay-as-you-go basis. I've only experimented very briefly with Instagram ads to date, and not enough to say how well they work. Once your book is selling well and has reviews, search online and read up on best practice and what is working for **children's authors** before being tempted to dip in your toe. Given that Instagram is part of the Facebook family I'd be wary of money getting eaten up!

3. Amazon Marketing Services (AMS)

Certainly the game-changer for many self-published authors in the last 18 months, including me, has been the ability to promote our books on Amazon, using Amazon Marketing Services (AMS). The service allows you to run pay-per-click ads for your book using 'sponsored product keyword advertising' or 'product display advertising'.

- If you're with KDP Print you can advertise both print and eBooks in the US through AMS via your KDP dashboard, under the 'Promote and Advertise' button. If you're with CreateSpace (being phased out) you can only advertise the eBook via KDP. My own and others' experience is that customers who respond to either ad mostly buy the print book.

- At the time of writing, in order to advertise in the UK, you need to sign up through the Amazon Advantage programme at **advantage.amazon.co.uk/ gp/vendor/sign-in** though this may change.

Sponsored product keyword advertising means paying to have your book show up in the search results or underneath the 'Customers also bought' list on a given book's sales page, in a row named 'Sponsored products related to this item'. Your book will only appear if a customer types in a search word or phrase that you've chosen to bid on *and* your bid 'wins' the auction for that keyword based on the price you bid. Keywords might be names of books or authors writing in a similar genre to you. Or they might be more general such as 'adventure book for kids'.

With **product display ads** you bid to have an ad for your book appear on the sales page for specific titles you select. You also have the option to allow Amazon to widen the reach of your ad to similar titles their algorithms consider to be a suitable match. Product display ads appear in a box below the blurb for a given book's sales page or just under its 'buy' button.

When you're next on Amazon take a look, and you'll see these ads running on just about every page you visit.

A level playing field for self-published books

The reason AMS has been such a game changer is two-fold.

- First, the visibility it gives our titles in the very place customers have come to browse and buy books – this is a whole different world from Facebook where users have so many other distractions.

- Second, it puts us on a level playing field with all publishers for promotion in a way that had been impossible to achieve previously. Think of the tables of books you see carefully arranged as you walk into Waterstones in the UK, Barnes & Noble in the US and any other bookstore chain where you live. Ditto the major bookstore chains' shop window displays. Publishers have huge influence over placement here, and sometimes pay good money for the privilege – way beyond what any indie author could afford, even if it were possible to get distribution into high street bookshops. The cost to run AMS ads is not prohibitive and is easy to control. In effect, Amazon has opened up its shop window and table space to everyone, and keeps it stocked based on what customers buy.

No matter what you bid for your keywords or related titles, if your book doesn't sell or get clicks, Amazon will in time stop showing your promotion – they firmly put their customers first. So if you have a great book, a great book cover and, ideally, a clutch of good reviews, you have as much chance as any other author of gaining sales through Amazon advertising – and it needn't break the bank.

How AMS has helped my sales

As I type *The Secret Lake* is ranked at 191 in the whole of the Amazon UK print store, having gradually crept up through the ranks since I first began AMS advertising in the UK in February 2018. It's also broken into the top 1,000 on Kindle in recent weeks.

It's always been my bestseller at school events and now that Amazon has allowed others to find it, it's proving itself all over again.

The sales spike may not last, but I'm enjoying it while it does and I hope you will indulge me here. I am thrilled that so many children are now enjoying this magical story – thank goodness I took it back out of that box in my office in 2010 after it had sat there for 10 years!

AMS advertising is definitely something to consider once your book is up and running. The full detail beyond this is outside the scope of this book and is something I may come back to in a specific guide for children's authors once I have more data from all advertising platforms I have tried.

Two tips I can give in the meantime are:

- research your keywords carefully and advertise against books and authors that are genuinely a good 'fit' with yours – this is where I seem to get the best results
- don't rule out the option for automatic targeting by Amazon – certainly in the UK this is producing good results for me and I'm not sure why I didn't try it sooner

As I previously mentioned, there's lots of free information out there if you search on Amazon, Google and Facebook – and it's covered in detail in the **Selfpublishingformula.com** 'Ads for Authors' course.

Also, listen to **Self-publishing Podcast Episode 128** where Canadian children's author Laurie Wright talks about the success she's had with AMS ads. You'll find this with a quick search on Google. (The follow-on **podcast 129** is with me and covers all aspects of children's publishing and marketing, ahead of the launch of this book.)

Further tip: You can use a tool called **KDP Rocket** to help with keyword search, albeit when using it for children's books I found myself having to unpick a lot of YA/adult titles from the results. However, the owner tells me this is being fixed in an upcoming release. On that basis it's certainly worth considering. It's also good for category research. The cost is $97. Many children's authors I know use it. Find out more or sign up via my affiliate link at **bit.ly/KDPRocketKaren** – or search online.

4. Pinterest advertising

Pinterest allows you to promote your pins in the same way that Facebook allows you to boost posts – and will encourage you to do so on the fly at the time of posting. They also have an ads dashboard from which you can plan and set up campaigns in advance. At the end of the day it amounts to the same thing – just approached through different doors.

Because the *The Secret Lake* has been doing well on Amazon, I've just decided to start experimenting with these ads to see if they can help me maintain my Amazon ranking. It's too early to say how well they are working, but I'm cautiously optimistic given the demographic.

I would suggest experimenting with organic pins and shares to start with and look to advertising only once you have reviews, and only if you think you need to. You may find that your organic pins serve you well enough. Since I've been so inactive on Pinterest over the last couple of years and the Amazon sales spike is happening now, I thought it best to strike while the iron was hot. But I may rein back to organic posting in due course once I've had time to analyse the results properly. Find out more at **pinterest.com**

5. BookBub advertising

Another potential advertising platform to consider once your book has reviews is BookBub, a website that promotes free or discounted eBooks to highly targeted (genre specific) lists of avid readers around the world. Authors and publishers can bid to run pay-per-click or pay-per-impression ads to go out with BookBub's newsletters, with the ads linking through to your sales page on your chosen platform. The ads are quick and easy to set up and you can stop and start them at any time.

At the time of writing I've only used BookBub sparingly and to very little avail at a high cost-per-click rate! However, this was before *The Secret Lake* hit the Amazon bestseller lists so I do plan to dip my toe in one more time. If I do get clicks at a reasonable cost, I shall be interested to see whether I gain print sales rather than eBook sales, which is what mostly happens with AMS.

Before trying out the BookBub ads platform, I'd highly recommend reading around on what works and how to avoid wasting money through inefficient targeting or the wrong bid rates. A good place to start is the **Self-publishing Podcast Episode 90 with Adam Croft** – found with a quick Google search. But search beyond this also, as things may have moved on since I last checked.

To understand more about how BookBub marketing works, go to: **support.bookbub.com**

25

EBOOK MARKETING: GO WIDE OR USE KDP SELECT?

When you come to upload your .mobi file to the Kindle Store, you will be given the option to enrol in Amazon's 'KDP Select' programme. This means you commit to making your eBook exclusive to Amazon for a period of 90 days and cannot sell it or give it away on any other store or website, including your own. In return, Amazon makes it available through its Kindle Unlimited subscription service, which allows readers to borrow and read unlimited eBooks from its library each month (either on a Kindle, or on other devices using the Kindle App).

With KDP Select, a 'borrow' counts towards your book's Kindle Store ranking and you are paid based on the number of 'page reads' each calendar month. How much you are paid per page read depends on the size of the KDP Fund, announced by Amazon after the end of each month and (I assume) based on the number of Kindle Unlimited subscriptions sold that month and other factors. The fund proceeds are split between all books enrolled in KDP Select that had page reads. At the time of writing, you are typically paid around 0.0045 cents per page read.

You can view the history of page-read payouts at: **writtenwordmedia.com/2018/05/18/kdp-global-fund-payouts**

Crucially, from a marketing perspective, KDP Select members are allowed to set their books 'free' for five days a month and use those days to market it*. Any free 'sales' made during that time qualify as 'verified purchases' for review purposes. Many authors use KDP free days to raise the profile of a new book or a back title as the free downloads often lead to paid sales in the days that follow.

I've only used the free days offer once back in 2014 – over two days for *Eeek! The Runaway Alien*. From memory there were around 7,000 downloads. However, I don't recall it leading to more reviews or more print book sales or paid eBook sales of any note – if it had I'm sure I'd have used it for other books. How typical my experience is I can't say I'm afraid!

*Remember: other than through KDP Select, Amazon doesn't let you price your eBooks as free, even though they may at their discretion price match if you have it free on another store.

Is KDP Select right for you?

This you need to weigh up and decide for yourself. I've moved my books in and out of KDP Select over the years and never sold many eBooks on the other platforms. However, other children's authors I know have found that setting an eBook free on several platforms has led to more print sales after Amazon prices matches and parents 'try for free' before they buy in print for their children. I think this may work especially well if you're writing a series, so is worth bearing in mind.

If you're planning to run AMS ads, my personal view is that you're probably better off 'in' than out of KDP Select to start with, whether or not you use their free promotion days, as I sense that 'algorithmic merchandising' may work in your favour as Amazon tries to gain more subscribers to Kindle Unlimited. (I should stress that this is just my hunch.) Whether that's a good or bad thing is another question but, at the end of the day, selling children's books is difficult if you're an unknown author without the backing of a publisher's marketing department. This is further compounded by the fact that the buyer isn't your reader.

You can, of course, move out of KDP Select after 90 days if you're not happy with the results. In fact, I've recently heard that if you write to them to ask to be released sooner they usually oblige!

For now, Amazon has become my marketing department and I believe (but can't prove) that KDP Select has helped in some way on that front. Ironically – and happily – this marketing effort is (as far as I can see) also leading to more print sales for bookshops and that can only be a good thing!

Search for **KDP Select** on Amazon for more information.

26

CHILDREN'S BOOK AWARDS OPEN TO SELF-PUBLISHED AUTHORS

One way you can help raise your book's profile is by winning an award (or being placed in the runners up or finalist shortlist) as this offers the chance for PR, winner stickers and more.

Yes, that's easier said than done – but you can't win if you don't try!

Overleaf you'll find example awards that are open to self-publishers and accept children's books. These have been checked and recommended as 'safe' by the Alliance of Independent Authors. Beyond this I'd say 'buyer beware'. You may come across others or receive marketing emails encouraging you to enter a specialist award – but take care. Some come with high fees and/or such a high number of categories that their key aim appears to be making money over and above highlighting great children's books.

Book awards vetted by the Alliance of Independent Authors and which accept children's books

- The Wishing Shelf Book Awards (thewsa.co.uk)
- The International Rubery Awards (ruberybookaward.com)
- The Kindle Storyteller Awards (search online)
- The Eric Hoffer Award (hofferaward.com)

(This list may be updated over time, so do check.)

If you are contemplating entering any other award, check ALLi's list first using the link below. ALLi rates most of the awards that are out there with commentary on whether to proceed with caution: **bit.ly/selfpubawards**

If this page should move at any future date, search for *Alliance of Independent Authors award and content ratings.*

I have personally entered The Wishing Shelf Book Awards – for which *Walter Brown and the Magician's Hat* was a Red Ribbon Winner (essentially a runners up award) – and would highly recommend it. Not only is your book read and voted on by children and teachers in UK primary schools, but you can also pay a small amount extra at entry to receive a written report on what did and didn't work, no matter where you come in the competition.

I regret not discovering this award sooner. Had I done so I'd certainly have entered *The Secret Lake* and *Eeek! The Runaway Alien.*

27

STRATEGIC MARKETING TIPS FOR CHILDREN'S AUTHORS

To round off, below is a very quick list of tips that may help you sell more books. Not all are unique to children's books and some I've covered already.

- Write a series – if you hook the reader in with book one they will come back for more. This is especially the case with children's books.

- If you write in a series and have a number of books, create an eBook version of the first one and list it for free on all the main eBook sites and at 0.99p / 0.99c on Amazon, then ask Amazon to price match. Several children's authors I know have reported success with crossover sales to print using this strategy. (Amazon won't allow you to price as free but if you use the button on your sales page to report the lower prices elsewhere they will usually price match to zero.)

- If you don't have a series, aim to write to the same age group and include an excerpt from one of your other books in your back matter.

- If you write across a range of age groups, turn it to your advantage – you have the opportunity to offer to see more pupils/classes at school visits. Also, most young children have siblings – so be sure to include the target age range when promoting your other books in your back matter.

- Once you have several books, consider creating an eBook that includes the first chapter of each and make this 99c/99p on Amazon and free on all other stores. I've done this with *Story Stack* – search online.

- Within the above eBook include links to each book's sales pages – and a link to a free download in return for signing up to your email list. (See below.)

- Offer something for free from your website or back of your book to encourage email sign-up and/or to hook new readers into your books. This might be a short story prequel to one of your books, a character's diary entry, or a quiz or puzzle that relates to the *theme* of your book. For younger audiences it could be downloadable colouring sheets. In all cases include the book title and URL of your website in the footer. If these freebies get passed around it could lead to more sales.

- Read up on how to select the most appropriate keywords and categories for your book on Amazon to make it discoverable – covered at: **kdp.amazon.com/en_US/help/topic/G200652170**

- Be sure to include the age range and US grade range, as these further improve discoverability. Use the link above or go to the KDP website, click on *Help* and look under *Publish your book > EBook Details/Paperback details.* Drill down through all relevant links on these pages. You'll find a table that lists the recommended age ranges and US grades, as well as a page outlining required keywords to fit in certain children's book categories. These keywords may change over time so I shall refrain from listing them here.

- Make the most of the fact that you can ask to be included in up to 10 categories in the Amazon Kindle Store and a similar number in the Books store. Identify the best categories for your book and call them or use the 'Contact us' button within KDP/CreateSpace to email your requests. Don't be tempted to opt for unsuitable categories just for the sake of inclusion or to try to win a 'bestseller' badge. This will confuse the Amazon algorithms, which may start recommending your book to unsuitable audiences and then downgrade its visibility in searches if sales don't follow. (Amazon will list the three categories where you rank highest in the 'Product details' section of your book page. Their bestseller rankings are updated hourly so your ranking and/or the categories displayed will change accordingly.)

- Claim and set up your Author page on Amazon.co.uk and Amazon.com – visit my author page and other author pages to get an idea of what to include. The instructions for how to set the page up are clear – just look for the link on your book's sales page once it appears on Amazon. Make the most of the opportunity to add links to your blog and social media. (If you can follow French, German and any other European language and have the time, set up your pages there too!)

- Read up on how to make your book blurb and Amazon page description compelling – listen to the **Indie Kidlit Podcast Episode 30 with Bryan Cohen** and search online for more interviews with him.

- Consider offering Skype classroom visits. A quick online search will throw up plenty of information. I have done this on a few occasions using the Microsoft Educator platform and shipped signed books abroad as a result.

- Once you have an established sales track record and testimonials from school visits, search online for organisations in your country that connect schools with authors. Most say they won't accept self-published authors, but they will make exceptions. In the UK am listed with the website *Contact An Author* – this was after three years into my school visits programme.

- Research audiobooks and story podcasting – outside the scope of this book but both growing markets for children's books.

Recommended reading on discoverability

A good place to start if you want to understand more about the principles of category choice and discoverability is *Let's Get Visible by David Gaughran*. (Published in 2013, so elements may be out of date, but the key messages still hold true.) David's later books *Let's Get Digital* and *Strangers to Superfans* are also recommended for further on in your marketing journey. His key messages – that asking friends and family to buy your book and/or placing your title in irrelevant categories in order to get a 'bestseller' tag are not ways to get your book noticed on Amazon (and indeed can positively harm its performance) – are always at the forefront of my mind when planning my marketing.

Popular tools to help with keyword and category selection

These tools were extremely helpful to me when first setting up AMS ads, though more recently I've been 'hand-picking' my keywords and categories. Prices as at July 2018.

- **KDP Rocket – $97 (bit.ly/KDPRocketKaren)**
- **Kindle Spy – $47** (search online)

WRITING AND SELF-PUBLISHING GROUPS AND WEBSITES

The self-publishing world is renowned for its generosity. Support from other children's writers and the wider self-publishing community can be a lifeline when you're struggling to understand why something isn't working, need best practice tips, are looking for feedback on book covers or descriptions, want advice on courses or other paid services and much more. Below are self-publishing organisations, groups, website and podcasts that I recommend.

Organisations

The Alliance of Independent Authors (ALLi)

The leading global professional association for authors who self-publish and which brings together the world's best indie authors, advisors and self-publishing services. ALLi champions professionalism in self-publishing and actively campaigns to protect, promote and further the interests of independent authors in the publishing world. Once you join you get access to its closed Facebook page, which you can drop into at any time to search for advice or ask a question.

allianceindependentauthors.org

If you decide to join please consider using the affiliate link **bit.ly/ALLiKaren** – I'll earn a small referral fee, but it won't cost you more. Thank you!

Society of Children's Book Writers and Illustrators (SCBWI)

A great networking organisation for children's authors including traditionally published, unpublished/looking for a traditional deal, and self-published. Headquarters are in the US but it has very active 'chapters' and Facebook pages in many countries including the UK, and annual conferences in the US and UK that are jam-packed with practical guidance on children's book writing and marketing. You don't need to be a member to attend the conferences.

SCBWI.org

Websites and podcasts for children's authors

Indie Kidlit Podcast

A regular podcast on all things children's book marketing, hosted by the children's and middle grade authors Marti Dumas in New Orleans and Elena Paige in Melbourne. Great fun, great guests and full of insights – highly recommended.

indiekidlitpodcast.com

Darcy Pattison website

US children's author Darcy Pattison is both traditionally and self-published. As well as writing for children she runs children's writing workshops and retreats. Visit her website for a wealth of information including periodic deep dives into the technical side of self-publishing. Darcy also has an online course on how to write and self-publish a children's picture book. **darcypattison.com**

Self-publishing Adventures website

As you will know, this is my own website, started back in 2011 soon after I began my self-publishing journey. It focuses on the practicalities of self-publishing and marketing children's books. At the time of writing it's sorely in need of an update, which I shall attend to once this book is out. In the meantime, the information it contains holds true and it still gets around 100 daily visits from around the world. A place to refer others looking for free guidance who may not be ready to buy this book. **selfpublishingadventures.com**

Websites and podcasts (self-publishing general)

Self-publishing Advice – Alliance of Independent Authors (ALLi)

This is the free advice blog of ALLi and is not to be missed. You don't have to be a member of ALLi to access the articles but you do need to be if you want to write for the blog or be featured. Filled with indispensable guidance on all aspects of self-publishing, broken down into handy sections. Use search to bring up specific children's book articles. **selfpublishingadvice.org**

The Creative Penn website and podcast

Self-publishing guru Joanna Penn's jam-packed website is full of free advice on self-publishing fiction and non-fiction, plus articles, interviews, free downloads, videos, free and paid-for training. She also hosts a regular podcast. Search 'children's books' on the site to focus on our genre – there's lots in there. **thecreativepenn.com**

Self-publishing Formula website and podcast

Thriller writer Mark Dawson and his team offer a wealth of free guidance on self-publishing as well as highly regarded paid-for online courses that have changed many authors' lives. A great resource for beginners and seasoned self-publishers alike, with access to a closed Facebook community group for mailing list members. Its scope is much wider than children's books, but it is not to be missed. **selfpublishingformula.com**

RESOURCES AND UPDATES

You will find all the downloads and key checklists that come with this book in a resources folder at the following hidden link:

selfpublishingadventures.com/resources

The password, which is case sensitive, is **WellSaidPress**.

I shall also use this folder to post news of changes in the self-publishing world that affect the currency of this book's content – and to add additional recommended resources that I come across. If you are signed up to my mailing list I shall also email you whenever I post there.

SELF-PUBLISHING: A CLOSING TALE

A few years ago one of the main UK publishers offered me a traditional publishing deal to write this book. It came after one of their editors had attended a presentation I gave on children's self-publishing as part of a creative writing workshop at a leading London literary agency.

I was heartened and pleased to see that the traditional publishing industry even back then was starting to take self-publishing seriously. Commercially driven royalty rates aside, however, my main concern was that the book would be out of date by the time the proposed seven-month writing schedule ran its course. This book has taken four months to write and each day I'm concerned about what's changed!

I also wanted to retain control of the project...

Where next for publishing?

I have feeling that as things continue to evolve we're all going to meet in the middle – as is already happening in the freelance editing, illustrating, layout and translating worlds. Marketing is up next and Sam Missingham (ex Harper Collins) is already blazing the trail on that front with **LoungeBooks.com** where she is using her publishing expertise and connections to help both traditionally published and self-published authors market their books and make more sales.

Meanwhile, at Thrillerfest 2018 in New York (a conference for thriller enthusiasts, readers, authors, and agents) the Self-publishing Formula team bagged a clutch of interviews with high-profile traditional authors including Lee Child, Lynda La Plante and David Morrell to name but a few.

As the traditional and self-publishing worlds continue to collide I'm hopeful that more ways of working together to create and promote top quality books will evolve, irrespective of route to publication. Needless to say, I include children's books in this mix. I hope that you are as excited as I am to be a part of this changing landscape!

REVIEW AND FEEDBACK

PLEASE LEAVE A SHORT REVIEW ONLINE

I hope you have found this book useful, wherever you are in your writing or publishing journey.

It would mean a lot to me if you could leave an honest review online – however short – every little helps, as we authors all know. **Thank you!**

FEEDBACK

If you want to alert me to a resource or service that you feel deserves a mention in the resources folder for this book, please email me and I'll take a look and get back to you as soon as I can.

You can contact me at: kpinglis@wellsaidpress.com

ALSO BY KAREN INGLIS

The Secret Lake (8-11 yrs)

A lost dog, a hidden time tunnel and secret lake take Stella and Tom to their home and the children living there 100 years in the past. Amazon UK bestseller summer 2018. Considered for CBBC TV.

Eeek! The Runaway Alien (7-10 yrs)

A soccer-mad alien comes to Earth for the World Cup! *"Laugh-out-loud funny!"* Loved by keen and reluctant readers alike. Voted favourite book club read three years in a row by boys and girls at one London primary school.

Walter Brown and the Magician's Hat (7-10 yrs)

A boy, a magic top hat and a talking cat spell magical mayhem after Walter Brown inherits his Great Grandpa Horace's magician's hat! *Wishing Shelf Awards* Red Ribbon Winner 2016.

Henry Haynes and the Great Escape (6-8 yrs)

A boy, a magic library book and a bossy boa – oh, and a VERY smelly gorilla with a zoo escape plan! Fun and fast-paced for early readers.

Ferdinand Fox's Big Sleep (3-5 yrs)

"Ferdinand Fox curled up in the sun, as the church of St Mary struck quarter past one..." A gentle rhyming fox tale, based on the true story of a fox that fell asleep in the author's garden.

Ferdinand Fox and the Hedgehog (3-6 yrs)

"As soon as she smelled the scent of a fox, she scampered to hide in an old soggy box." Introducing Hatty the hedgehog and her baby son Ed. Includes eight pages of photos and fun facts about foxes and hedgehogs.

Order online or from your local bookshop

ABOUT THE AUTHOR

Karen Inglis is an Amazon UK bestselling children's author (2018) who lives in London, England. She has two sons who inspired her to write when they were younger. Karen has presented on children's self-publishing at conferences and masterclasses around the UK and is Children's Advisor at the Alliance of Independent Authors. For her **non-fiction** she writes under the name **Karen P Inglis**.

Sign up to her mailing list at
selfpublishingadventures.com/news to follow her journey
and be notified about **updates or additions to this book.**

Sign up to her children's books mailing list at
kareninglisauthor.com to be notified about **new children's
book releases, events and special offers.**

 facebook.com/kareninglisauthor
 twitter.com/kareninglis
 instagram.com/kareninglis_childrensbooks

ACKNOWLEDGEMENTS

Huge thanks to my editor Catherine Gough of **FineWords.net** for her attention to detail and useful comments over so many pages. Also to Rachel Lawston of **LawstonDesign.com** for the cover concept and design. Needless to say, both come highly recommended!

Also thanks to all my blog followers – and to fellow children's authors and self-publishers in the various online groups to which I belong and with whom I have exchanged so much know-how over the years. The indie author community is a very special one where we are all constantly learning from each other and I feel privileged to be a member.

34176425R00166

Made in the USA
San Bernardino, CA
30 April 2019